THE FRUITS OF EDEN

A book about the Book

Simon Praamsma

SQUARE CIRCLES PUBLISHING

THE FRUITS OF EDEN
A book about the Book

© 2015 Simon Praamsma
www.SiemPraamsma.com

Cover design: Syrp & Co.
Cover illustration: Simon
Political map image: Shutterstock.com

SQUARE CIRCLES PUBLISHING
P.O. Box 9682, Pahrump
NV 89060 U.S.A.
www.SquareCirclesPublishing.com

ISBN: 978-0-9905813-8-3
eISBN: 978-0-9905813-9-0

CONTENTS

AUTHOR'S NOTE vii
    Introduction to the Book ix
    Use of the words Yahweh, Government, Religion,
        Planet and World in this book xi
    Disclaimer. xii

THE FRUITS OF EDEN 1
    The Book 1
    Spirit 3
    Belief. 5
    Atoms 6
    Common sense scientific assumptions
        and observations. 7
    Design 10
    Living cells. 11
    The Big Bang and the Phantom 11
    The Brain 17
    Learning. 18
    Recognition 19
    Mental metabolism. 20
    Myth and tradition 21
    Monotheism. 22
    The people. 23
    The God 25
    Opposition 26
    How Holy the Spirit 28
    "Planet" and "World". 31
    A promise 32
    The snake that talked. 32
    Strange punishment 33

Eve Ate: A short history of *un*civilization 33
Creation: Beginning 34
The Man 36
Eve 39
Eve's compassionate spirit 39
The start of our world 42
Genetically Modified Organisms (GMOs),
    one of the later fruits of Eden. 42
True and false religious thinking 43
Taking the Name in vain. 44
Cain and Abel. 45
The role of a herder 46
Adam and Eve—Realization 1. 47
Adam and Eve—Realization 2: The naked truth 48
Civilization or *un*civilization 49
Why does Religion exist in the first place? 50
Moses and the God. 53
A mystery 54
Pitfalls of power. 55
Stories and phantasms 56
The Chosen 58
Noah 59
The rainbow significance. 62
The diet adjustment 62
Noah's legacy 62
The nature of Religion 63
The Big Lie, BIGGEST fruit of all 65
 Life after death, and angels 69
Good and bad People 71
Immortal soul. 72
Sin, one of the early fruits of Eden 74
The wicked 76
Why does the Devil do this? 82
Violence 82
Jesus the redeemer 83
Other sources of information about Jesus 83

Jesus, the story 84
Consider the temptation. 86
Wilderness metaphor. 86
Killed by Religion. 88
The need for damage control 89
The Book of Revelation, the Apocalypse. 93
Misinformation. 93
666 94
Money and the commercial system. 95
The Government/Religion combination 96
Government or no government. 98
The Crusades 102
The newest invention—the Rapture 103
Religion 105
The Inquisition 106
Misinformation Clearing House/Satan 108
The evil monster sanitized. 109
Organized Religion's inspiration. 109
The real Satan 110
Jehovah's Witnesses and the Book 111
The World today 114
War as a business, a bitter fruit 119
Yahweh—in conclusion 120
A real theocracy. 121
God or no God, what would it take? 123
Stephen Hawking. 124
Big Bang revisited. 125

SOME EXPLANATIONS. 128
   The snake and his strange punishment, or the fate of Satan .128
   Revelations 20:10 describes Satan's final end 129

BIBLE REFERENCES OF INTEREST 131

ACKNOWLEDGMENTS 132

"All national institutions of churches,
whether Jewish, Christian or Turkish,
appear to me no other than human inventions,
set up to terrify and enslave mankind,
and monopolize power and profit."

—*Thomas Paine,* The Age of Reason *(1794).*

AUTHOR'S NOTE

This book is not the result of a couple of months' writing, or even a couple of years. It came into being in the course of about twenty-five or thirty years, whenever I had the opportunity to spend a few minutes—first with pen and paper, then at my typewriter, later on my word processor, and finally at my computer. Family circumstances made it impossible to spend more than that at my writing. I never saw my efforts as leading to a book, a focused effort concentrated on a goal such as this.

My formative years in the Netherlands, from 1927 to 1938, included a primary school where the Bible was part of the curriculum. Although my parents were basically anti-religion, my father's parents were churchy people and paid the extra fees involved. It was often confusing for a six-year-old. From nine to four I was supposed to be devout, but after 4 o'clock derision about religion from my father took over. Because of this, I ended up with a fairly good knowledge of the fundamentals of religion and the Book it was supposedly based on, plus a healthy dose of doubt about both.

The Second World War came and towards the end of it I was hiding from the German Occupation in a small village, where I read every available book in the house until there was nothing left but a Bible, which I wasn't eager to start on. But eventually boredom won over. Now on my own, without institutional "guidance," I was amazed to find how different the content was from what I had been taught. The fact that we had landed in a brutal war may have had something to do with it. An inkling of the Bible's purpose began to form in my mind. My outlook on life changed and has so remained.

Not until I turned thirty or thereabouts did I realize that there was something seriously wrong with the world—and certainly with its so-called spiritual aspect. But thirty is not an age when one thinks too deeply about things; at that age more immediate and seemingly more important matters take priority. However, when in my late fifties I was forced to stay in bed with a serious attack of the flu, I acquired a small yellow pad and a ballpoint pen and began in earnest, writing under the blankets while I had a temperature of over a hundred degrees.

When I later read it back, what I had written did not seem to be the result of feverish imagination. I kept it until I had my Canon Bubble Jet word processor/printer, when I was able to save it onto a floppy disc. In the course of the years more floppies followed, which in due time I was able to transfer to my first computer.

I did not write for an audience, because I didn't have an audience. My family and friends were not all that interested. Moreover, the subject matter was not to everybody's liking, especially the articles about Religion.

I wrote for myself, is what it amounted to. I wanted to put my thoughts and conclusions about what I found in the Book on paper to read it back now and then, to reinforce the conviction that had formed in my mind and also to see if I needed to make a change in my understanding of the worldly things around me. It surprises me, when reading something I wrote twenty-five years ago, that hardly anything has fundamentally changed since I wrote it.

I had started a computer file named "State of the World Articles," and the idea of turning the dozen or so articles into a book began to crystallize. About a year ago I began to seriously work on it. However, when I started researching in earnest I had no idea that the tenor of the book would not turn out the way I had expected it to. My opinion about the dark role of Religion in our daily affairs did not change, neither did the part Government played. What I had not foreseen was that the book would seriously question the role of Science and the sanity of some of its highly respected scientists. Even the authority of Einstein came to be challenged.

I found that certain scientists had called the generally accepted view of Creation—with its official view of Gravity, the Big Bang and the theory of relativity—"the Preposterous Universe," and I understood why. The origin and actual age of the Universe, and the role of stars and planets, became open to doubt. It was also clear that the guardians of the official scientific view do not tolerate dissent about it.

Then there was the veracity of the Book—the Bible—itself that did not quite come up to expectations. Because of the Eden story of eating forbidden fruit in Genesis, the very first book of the Book, it seemed appropriate to name my book *The Fruits of Eden* because everything that had transpired since was related to that remarkable happening, the consumption of the wrong foodstuffs.

Introduction to the Book

For those who don't own a Bible, or those who do and have rarely opened it, this book may be hard to understand. But it does not have to be. Of course it would be to the reader's advantage to have a minimum familiarity with the stories in it, but for those who don't I have cited the passages in the Book where a reader can look them up. The Book is a hefty tome—there are a lot of pages to deal with. I used a variety of versions: the King James Translation; an old Dutch version from 1934 which is hardly readable today because of its archaic language; the Internet; the New World Translation by the Watchtower Bible and Tract Society, mainly because someone gave me a copy and I found its use of everyday language helpful; and others. Depending on the formatting the number of pages varies from over 900 to 1600-plus.

When comparing the various translations it is also clear that even here bias is not far away. The New World Translation, published by the Jehovah's Witnesses sect, puts heavy emphasis on *"the system of things,"* a term not used in other translations, although there is no doubt about its meaning: the way the world is run.

Because of its size, at first it seems like a mountainous task to find anything in the Book. However, it is put together in such a way that it is very easy to track down a certain sentence or thought. The first few pages usually contain an index with the names of the books and their page numbers. For example: 2 Peter 3:8 means the second book of Peter, chapter 3, line 8, which will tell you that to The God, one day is like a thousand years, and a thousand years is as one day.

Nowadays I rely more and more on the internet, where you can look up a certain passage in the Book and compare it with a dozen other translations, eliminating the necessity of having ten or twenty different versions on your bookshelf. If you do not want to possess a Bible, and do not want to be seen with one in your hand, but you have a computer, all you have to do is type 2 Peter 3:8 in your browser and your machine will come up with the desired info. Or if you don't know who Abraham is, type in "Abraham Bible" and Google will do the rest.

I have purposely not given Bible references in all instances, because I did not want to create the impression that this is a religious tract, which it certainly is not, and also because I have found that it interferes with the rhythm of reading. And wherever I have cited a passage without further explanation, it is because I want to tease the reader into looking it up for himself, as for example Revelations 12:9.

Don't be put off if your Bible is written in what seems to be an ancient language, like my sometimes incomprehensible Dutch version. That writing style was maintained for the same reason that nuns and monks were dressed for a long time in clothes belonging to the Middle Ages, and why God was often pictured with a long white beard—to impress the reader or onlooker with the seriousness and age of the message.

However, there are now plenty of versions of the Book available which have done away with the "thy" and "thou" and "ye" and give you plain words in your everyday language.

The Book is not a novel. With its symbolism it is a storehouse of knowledge and wisdom, but finding the knowledge, and discerning where its wisdom is located takes scrutiny and reflection.

Use of the words Yahweh, Government, Religion, Planet and World in this book

In this book we use the term "The God" or "Yahweh" (for ease of pronunciation) when referring to YHWH, to avoid confusion with any other gods. There is uncertainty about how this should be pronounced, due to a peculiarity of the Hebrew written language. Some prefer Yahweh, some Yahwih, again others Jehovah. The Hebrews themselves do not know either, because of a superstition attached to mentioning the name.

The word "Government," as it is used in this book, does not pertain to any particular government on earth. Neither does it point to a particular *form* of government, such as a Democracy, a Dictatorship, or a Theocracy. It is used generically. It is meant to express the wish to rule, manage, regulate, manipulate and sometimes exploit people.

The word "Religion" as used in this book encompasses all belief systems: the Jewish religion, Christianity, Islam, Buddhism, Theism, as well as the thousands of splinter sects and groups. The term is not meant to degrade any particular form of worship, but to include them all. It too, is used generically.

Whenever the word "World" is capitalized, it stands for the present way the world is ruled; its political and religious systems.

There is the World and there is the *Planet*. The Planet is the solid ball we live on. The way we live on it is called the World. The World is an intangible; an idea or a system implemented. The World exists on the planet.

Disclaimer

No claim is made, in this book about the Book, that any of the writings in it constitute truth or untruth; it will only report what the Book says, sometimes what it doesn't say, regardless of pronouncements by "experts," who often have an axe to grind. It is up to the individual to see what seems reasonable and what seems to be no more than fiction. Fiction has its place in education. The parables of Jesus are an example. Part of acquiring accurate knowledge is the ability to separate fact from fiction.

Pleasant reading!

SIMON PRAAMSMA
Pahrump, Nevada
April 2015

In the Garden of Eden story, in Genesis, the first book in the Book, we read of a snake talking a woman into eating a certain fruit that had been forbidden to her by Yahweh, The God, for she would die if she ate it. The snake then convinced her that she would not die, but become as wise as God.

THE FRUITS OF EDEN

The Book

The Prophet Mohammed, founder of Islam, called the Hebrews "people of the Book," meaning that they always carried with them what is called the Old Testament, the section of the Book that deals mainly with the fortunes and misfortunes of the descendents of Heber and their relationship with their Protector, the Almighty. A second part, the New Testament, developed, which covers the story of a man named Jesus and his twelve apostles. The two parts together are now known as the Bible, the word of God, the book that Christianity is supposedly based on. If this is true, then the Book is no longer the sole possession of the Hebrews—or Jews, as they are now called—and can be of interest to a much wider audience.

Because of the Book's claim that it is the word of God, it has become an object of controversy. Not everyone is convinced that a God exists in the first place, and, even if he did, they doubt that he would take the trouble to write a book, or have it ghostwritten in his name. Others, learning of the blood shed in the world by Christians in the past, want nothing to do with him.

Ingrained ideas about what the Book contains, what could be called the official view, have many people convinced that they already know what it is all about. They are put off by the mention of heaven and hell, angels and the Devil—all fables from a bygone era. Others believe that it belongs in a museum, the stories totally irrelevant in this modern day and age, especially when told in such antiquated language.

And then there are the disenchanted ones who were born into a religious sect and forced to believe the sect's dogmas, some of which were not necessarily based on the Book itself. Often, after leaving their particular church for good, they too joined the ranks of those who permanently shied away from opening the Book again. They do not see the necessity for reliving their aversion—or even revulsion—for all things religious, convinced it is all hogwash. They consider themselves emancipated, modern and free. If I had thought to direct this book to any group in particular, it would probably be them because of our similar disheartening experience.

There is certainly enough controversy swirling around this Best Seller to make one wonder what it is really about. Questions come up, such as: Is the Bible a reliable history book? Does it belong to Organized Religion? Who are the writers? What is inspiration? What is a prophet?

The contributors are called prophets claiming to be inspired to put into writing what God's intentions are for the planet and its inhabitants; sometimes the authors are known, sometimes not. Often symbols are used to convey a particular point, or when the author deems it necessary to emphasize that he means to generalize, or to suggest future happenings.

The Merriam-Webster dictionary defines "inspiration" as "something that makes someone want to do something, or that gives someone an idea about what to do, or create. A force or influence that inspires someone." Also, "Divine influence on a person believed to be qualified to receive sacred revelation." In such a case, it is of course important to know who does the qualification.

Because God is a spirit, and not visible—at least not to us—he cannot talk face-to-face with a human being; he needs a vehicle, or "voice," to relay his intentions to the world. Such a voice is often referred to as a prophet, and his message is a prophecy. The dictionary defines "prophecy" as: 1. An inspired utterance of a prophet; 2. The function or vocation of a prophet; specifically the inspired declaration of divine will and purpose; and 3. The prediction of something to come. In the case of the Book, a prophet is a spokesperson for Yahweh, who admonishes his people to stay away from the world's false gods and to put their trust in him only, warning of dire consequences if they ignore the exhortations.

Gods are spirit and do not speak audibly to people. A person may become aware that he or she entertains a certain spirit of thought and decide that such a spirit is telling him things. Those who say that a god spoke to them face to face are always alone—no one else is there to listen in and verify the phenomenon.

Spirit

A spirit could be compared to a thought. As we think, a thought forms in the mind. We contemplate and perceive it as beneficial or harmful, something to stay with or to leave alone. As a prophet thinks and gains insight into what his God is all about, he then speaks, or writes, in the spirit of his God. He *reveals* his God. It is well to remember that true revelation can never be in disagreement with human reason and experience.

Prophets are not fortune tellers; they observe the world around them, and the insight they gather in the course of their lives tells them that the world's political system, with its many "nations," is severely flawed, and on a path of destruction that cannot continue forever. In a quest for the cause of this phenomenon, one deduction led to another and finally to a conclusion. Their insight alerts us to the existence of, firstly, oppression by illegitimate world power; secondly, false or fake religion—its complement; and thirdly, loss of our right to life in the next world setup. Further contemplation led to the certainty that their God is capable of eventually ridding us of all three curses.

The Book calls it *the times of the end:* a day in the future when Yahweh promises to do away with the present ways and take over the reins. It calls it the Kingdom *of* Heaven. That day is not specified except that certain indications or signs will alert the world's population that it is imminent. Symbolic language is often used to describe the demise of the present system.

Some of the Book's writers were priests or prophets, others were farmers or tradesmen. When they acted as prophets they often denounced the misuse of power and the mistreatment of the downtrodden, predicting deliverance from oppression. They were not always well received, often meeting with fierce resistance or violence—sometimes deadly—from those who were on the side of the oppressors, misled into accepting the established ways of the world in general, often by their own family members.

It seems that the warnings were not meant for their contemporary Jews only; they appear to be directed at the far future and at a much wider world audience: *the aforementioned times of the end*, when Yahweh promises to do away with the present system and retake the reins.

Although Religion has more or less taken over the task of explaining the "mystery" of the Book, it is by no means certain that a mystery exists. It is clear that Organized Religion does not welcome a new world *on earth*, preferring to tell its members that this Kingdom will take place *in heaven*, almost immediately after death. There is a reason for this divergent train of thought, and it is made clear in this book.

It is remarkable that this difference of opinion can exist. If not symbolically used, the words in the Book are usually plain and simple; any hidden meaning discovered by the experts may have been added by them, sometimes in translation from the original. Copying the texts could also be the cause of "mistakes," if that is what they were.

It is often difficult for Organized Religion to adjust its views to those of the Book, which at times contradict its very dogmas.

Bypassing the simple utterances of the prophets, much of what Organized Religion tells us today about death and dying, including what happens next, was manufactured in Babylon thousands of years ago. Later on, pagan Greek interpretations were added, all very likely by persons who claimed a kinship with those who wrote the Book, by also claiming to have an "in" with whatever they considered to be God. Babylon, in the Book, is a metaphor for the World, its way of governing and its wayward religious beliefs.

In the Book of Revelation, the last book in the Book, the name "Whore of Babylon" has been given to Organized Religion, because she "fornicates with the nations." Religion in those days was so close to Government that it didn't matter. It is therefore entirely possible that any Babylonian information given was slanted in favor of the ruling classes who usually justify their political power through divine authority, handed to them by their priests.

It appears that present-day Religion treats many of those fabricated ancient pronouncements as the truth. This is not surprising as we discover that even today the interests of Government and Organized Religion overlap. By using our brains we should be able to learn the difference between what is reasonable and what is not.

That is what this book about the Book is all about. It will certainly offend many, because it goes against the accepted belief systems. It has nothing good to say about conventional Religion, Government and the way we treat the environment. If you don't agree with its findings and conclusions, don't worry. You are not alone.

Belief

The general definition of "belief" is *the full acceptance of a thing as true.*

To believe is a matter of trust—to have faith in, or trust, or regard as true something that cannot be physically perceived or proven by conventional scientific tests. However, other scientific facts may lead us to a conclusion, which then could be labeled "belief."

There are phenomena around us that we cannot comfortably ignore or explain away as self-evident. We can *see* that plants grow, that living things exist and that weather takes place. We may not understand why and how, but we cannot escape visual facts. There is no *belief* involved here; observation and the sense of touch will do the trick. What we cannot readily grasp are the how, the why, and maybe the who or the what. *What* makes plants grow, *how* do living things stay alive and *why* do we need "bad" weather?

Atoms

Science tells us that every object in the universe, even the most distant star, is made of atoms. Atoms are too small to see, but, when packed together, make up all kinds of chemical elements. We now know that every atom has a nucleus with a number of electrons that move around it. The simplest one, hydrogen, has one proton in its nucleus and one electron moving around it. Though hydrogen is the least complicated element in terms of protons and electrons, it fuels stars like our sun and is therefore vital to life.

There are 92 elements known to exist on earth, every one with its own atomic number, relating to the amount of electrons in its make-up. This pattern is the *Periodic Table*.

Even a slight change in the arrangement of atomic particles yields a different element. Where hydrogen has one electron, helium has two, lithium three, beryllium four, boron five, carbon six, nitrogen seven, oxygen eight, fluorine nine, neon ten, and so on down the list. Uranium, with 92, is at this time the last element found on earth. It is remarkable that some elements are solid and visible, while others are gaseous and invisible. Nevertheless, they all exist, neatly in their rank. Gold is number 79 and silver is number 47.

Everything in the universe follows rules described by the laws of physics (see *Encyclopedia of Stars and Atoms*[1]). According to currently accepted scientific dogma an *electromagnetic force* keeps an electron moving around the nucleus of an atom. Electrons would no longer be bound to atoms if this force was weakened, and we would have a universe where no chemical reactions would be possible. This balance is extremely delicate. This electromagnetic force is about 100 times weaker than the strong nuclear force that holds together the nuclei of atoms.

There are alternatives to the accepted common knowledge about these forces, but for the purposes of this book the end result is the same.

Common sense scientific assumptions and observations

Contrary to what mainstream scientists tell us, the "void" they refer to is not *empty*. By definition a void is an empty space, indicating an area that can be filled. This particular void has been filled with a *substance*, a massive ocean of energy, but because "modern" science chooses not to be aware of it, it has never been given an official name. Lacking that, I venture to speculate that it is the universal, lubricating transportation medium, because all forces need a medium "carrying" them from one place to another, and all heavenly bodies—suns, stars, planets and even galaxies—sail through it without friction. Gravity by itself does not play a role here.

The individual particles of this substance are so small that an atom, too small for us to see, placed next to it, would loom huge—almost like a solar system by comparison. Worldly measurements such as miles, inches, kilometers and centimeters

---
[1] Stuart Clark, *Encyclopedia of Stars and Atoms*, Andromeda Oxford Ltd., 1995).

are totally inadequate to express dimensions of this magnitude.

With the methods at our disposal at this time the existence of this substance defies detection, and can only be imagined, but this does not mean that it is solely a product of the imagination. It is, in effect, a scientific *necessity*; it *must* exist to transmit forces across expanses of space, be they infinitely large or infinitely small. Deductive reasoning is needed to explain a medium of this kind.

Although infinitesimally small, the individual particles of this medium are the energized building blocks of the visible universe. All matter consists of this material. *We* are made of it.

At one time, the substance had been given a name, "ether," but its existence was thought not to be provable. About a hundred years ago, conventional science abandoned further studies and pronounced it non-existent. Such a bold pronouncement, however, does not mean that scientists are right, or more trustworthy than brilliant minds of the recent past, who had deduced that it *had* to exist. Even Isaac Newton, admitting that he could not quite understand gravity, suspected the existence of a carrier medium.

Gravity is seen by conventional science as a *force*, an attraction between physical objects, where a smaller one is "falling" onto a larger one, through completely empty space, whether separated by enormous distances or relatively close to each other. However, contrary to this claim, mass does not have the property of mutual attraction. It is hard to understand that conventional science sticks to this dogma. Because if this were so, the universe would have become one giant, solid ball of matter eons ago. It would mean that each atom is capable of affecting other atoms, whether close by or billions of light years apart.

In reality, the ether (for lack of an official description) is being manipulated as we speak, producing elementary particles like neutrons, protons and electrons, in that order, the stuff atoms and elements are made of. "Solid" elements are dynamic structures of elementary particles, taking part in a continuous process of renewal, a never ending cycle, which takes place so rapidly that the elements seem unchanged to us, even for eons of time (as in rocks, for example), but are in effect in a state of perpetual youth. It makes one think that, if it can happen to rocks, why couldn't it happen to us?

The structures can be destroyed, but the ether particles that they are made with are indestructible and return to the "pool" when released.

Atoms have a nucleus around which electrons orbit. The element hydrogen has one proton and one electron, and is therefore the simplest element. More complex elements need neutrons for stability.

The number of protons and electrons is equal, but the number of protons and neutrons is not. Neutrons are unstable in their free state and decay in 1010 seconds (less than 17 minutes) into protons and electrons. Hydrogen is therefore the most abundant element in the universe. Stars make heavier elements, converting hydrogen to helium, then lithium and beyond, producing heat in the process. To think that this situation has come about by chance and is not the result of *design* may be a foolish notion, because, were this not so, or even slightly different, carbon atoms (#6 in the periodic table, symbol "C") could not exist. No life would be possible, carbon representing 20% of the weight of all living organisms.

Scientific facts have nothing to do with whether we believe them or not. There is nothing to stop us believing, for example, that this finely tuned arrangement has come about by chance. However, it is probably more prudent to accept the fact that the laws of nature were the result of Design. And when one comes to accept this, one must logically conclude that there is a *Designer*. That life came into existence without the active guidance of a highly intelligent Force is simply unthinkable.

Design

A designer is not someone with a magic wand which he waves in the air and creates something out of nothing, and The God is no exception. Designing is usually done in a sequence of stages. Creating any kind of artifact requires planning, knowledge, research, thought, sketches, notes, blueprints, testing, refining—all under the direction of the designer and possibly his assistants.

Technical rationality is always at the center of the process and any design is subject to the application of scientific and mathematical principles: the laws of nature.

A prototype is usually made and tested to see if it performs the task it was designed for. This is usually the time to observe if modifications need to be made.

A template can be constructed, so that final products will all have the same characteristics—say, four limbs, the possibility for a tail, a head with ears, eyes and mouth, and hands and feet shaped to make the best use of its environment. Then it could end up as a sheep, a goat, a dinosaur, a lion, an ape, a fish or a bird, or a human being. The fins of a fish and the wings of a bird are adapted limbs.

Future changes are considered and must then be incorporated in the setup. A scale model can be made to see if the design works according to expectations. If not, critical rethinking must take place until the desired goal has been reached. In short, a design needs a Mind capable of doing the job.

Our brain, however, has the capability to imagine alternative possibilities. If we shrink back from the idea that God the Designer exists, we can think, "Why couldn't the cosmos, the stars, the earth and humans have come about by a sequence of events *without* the involvement of a designer?" It doesn't seem likely, but there is nothing to stop us from imagining.

Living cells

The simplest living cell with a size of one millionth of a meter is intricate beyond imagining. It is a veritable macro-miniaturized factory containing thousands of elegantly designed pieces of molecular machinery far more complicated than any man-made structure. The best computer on earth is an inadequate, crude and clumsy product compared to even the smallest piece of a living cell. There can be no doubt that a cell is the result of an extremely well-planned design.

We can reason to ourselves that nature is definitely capable of making even a minute part of such a structure without the managed application of scientific and mathematical principles, relying on one particular chance occurrence after another. Such reasoning does not mean anything and neither does it change anything.

However, with our limited understanding and knowledge we cannot even perceive that an awesomely intelligent Power like an invisible designing God could exist. Our arrogance and sense of importance dictates that if *we* cannot create life, nobody can. We are, after all, the center of the universe, aren't we? Therefore, life must have come about by chance.

The Big Bang and the Phantom

It's not for us to say whether the scientists of our age are right or wrong about the universe. We have no way of disproving their conclusions one way or another. This is partly because we don't have access to the array of tools and instruments they use to come to their findings.

However, what seems odd is that in watching a documentary about the Big Bang, one gets the impression that a great explosion was all it took to create the wonderful, ordered, balanced universe—that there was no planning, no thought behind it. It seemed as if it was not pre-ordained at all—it was a remarkable happening that produced a most remarkable result. Either the rules of nature prevailing in the vast empty space made the debris clump into spheres, naturally going into orbits around other spheres, or it was a great coincidence that produced billions of suns, stars and planets. Magnetism played an important role, we learn. But did it?

The above scenario is indeed hard to believe. It seems appropriate to give it the name, "the Preposterous Universe." As a rule, explosions do not create order, they destroy it. The knowledge to determine in advance where the various bits and pieces of a cataclysm will end up, and as what, would be difficult to find in anyone's brain. However, the Doppler Effect, and the Red Shift seem to indicate that this particular explosion was a magical exception to the rule. C is the result of B, and B follows A. If A is a Bang, and B is a Red Shift, then C must be the Doppler Effect. Therefore it is now agreed by almost all of today's scientists that our planet is part of an ever-expanding universe. It is today accepted as universally true and basic knowledge by everyone else. But is it?

The universe is flying apart and it has so far not shown any signs of stopping. It is agreed that this is the normal result of any violent event of this kind, and certainly if it took place where it did. Some explosions just keep going for eons, and apparently this is one of them. Scientists even hear the echo of the original "BOOM!" From what solid edifice the sound bounced off is apparently not known, or has not yet been contemplated. The scientific community is mum about it, maybe for good reasons. It would, after all, turn out to be *the greatest discovery ever*, or at least of the last several billion trillion years, to find that, unbeknownst to any scientist on earth, solid matter existed before the BANG. It only goes to show that this particular explosion was not just any everyday car bomb—it was unique in so many ways.

Well . . .

No regular explosion will ever result in a predictably orderly array of usable parts. Try to explode something and see. Don't try this at home, but get a copy of the sheet music of Schubert's composition *Ave Maria*, this handsomely crafted combination of chords and melody. Cut all the notes from the paper, put them in a bag, throw in the chord symbols and add an explosive device. Then blow it up. Assuming that the ingredients survive, what chance is there that the notes will re-assemble themselves in the previous orderly procession, or even in any orderly procession, and that the chords are likely to find their place in the right spot where they do the most good to the original or the new melody? One in several trillion? Quazillion? Megazillion?

Schubert was a craftsman as well as a genius. He knew what he was doing, having thoroughly studied his subject matter until he was ready to proceed confidently with the task at hand. He most likely first heard the melody in his head, knew by experience which chords would harmonize, and knew exactly how to put it on paper. Something like that does not happen by chance. He *knew*. His brain had developed in such a way that he, with the right effort, could produce a most favorable result.

Now, what do you think would be a likely scenario for *someone* creating the universe, having a huge explosion ending up like it did, with everything in it perfectly interacting? Ah! But now you are introducing a *God*, you say. *We* are talking *Science! You* are talking *Religion!*

Religion? *Religion!?* What does Religion have to do with a Creator? Conventional or Organized Religion is a phantom, a tale concocted by long-forgotten rulers, who hoped to contain or even eliminate the violent streak in their subjects. They invented a fake soul, a fake heaven, a fake hell, a fake afterlife—the result of their imaginings they could not foresee. The creators of Religion did not have the required know-how to predict the consequences of their fabrications: an ever-more violent world. An imitation world.

Organized Religion is found in the lyrics to the *Ave Maria* composition, proclaiming the false notion of dead people gathering in a "heaven," even talking to God and putting in a good word on our behalf. Even though this official view of things by Religion as well as Government is accepted as truth by millions, it is not supported by anything in the Book, which is supposed to be the basis for the dogmas they present. It appears that opinions, suggestions and speculations presented in different books have been accepted by Organized Religion as more trustworthy, and maybe more universally acceptable.

We live in a violent world, and it may therefore not be a surprise to see noted scientists of our age coming to the conclusion that a great explosion was the cause of the universe coming into being. Violence has become such an accepted way of life in the present world that it pervades our thinking and perception of what is normal. Any other suggestion would lead by necessity to the idea that a certain someone, perhaps with peaceful intentions, was instrumental in the creation. A Creator. A Genius. "Someone" with the knowledge and unlimited power and time to accomplish what he intended to do. That, of course, would lead mainstream Scientists to conclude, uncomfortably, that thusly they'd be connected to what they, and 90% of the population, *think* of as Religion, not realizing that they are dealing with a phantom, a fake, a hoax. An unbridgeable gulf exists between Organized Religion and a Designer.

Therefore, in a contorted and limited way, they are right. Imitation religion has nothing to do with the creation. Or with the Creator, for that matter.

It is deplorable that Organized Religion exists in the form it does, and that it is confused with what one might call True Religion: an expression of appreciation, wonderment and admiration for a genius Creator.

Recognizing the hand of a Creator in the Bang would certainly result in better Science. But it would never result in contaminating it with Religion.

The journal *Search*, published by the Australian and New Zealand Association for the Advancement of Science (ANZAAS), contained the review of a 1980 book, *The Origin of Life*,[2] which described how life could have become about by chance. Author Hoyle lists "16 highly speculative statements, each depending on the preceding one for credence." He concluded that it was far easier to accept a Creator than to accept the myriad "blind chances" needed to support the thesis in the aforementioned book.

The German physicist Max Planck said, in 1944: "A Force, an intelligent Mind, brings the particles of an atom to vibration and holds it together. This Mind is the matrix of all matter."

So what is one to believe? If there is a Designer, it is probably a good idea to try to live in harmony with his universal laws. It is by now a well-established fact that disregarding these laws leads to disaster. Our conceited ideas on how to run the planet, for example, have so far produced overpopulation, pollution, health epidemics, destruction of the environment, poisoning of the water and the soil, climate change and a general reduction in the quality of life.

We can, however, *believe* in this system. There is nothing to stop us believing that "God" *wants* us to behave as we do. We can believe that our kings, presidents, dictators and sundry other rulers have been appointed by this Deity and believe that they have our best interests at heart. We can believe our Religious Leaders when they tell us that they have read in the Book that we'll go to heaven after we die, even if there is no mention of it. And we are also free to believe those who claim that we will end up on some far-away planet to be re-educated until we get it right. There is plenty of "fruit" to satisfy everyone.

We can believe those who say that "God" loves us no matter what, that we'll all be okay in the end and that no harm will

---

[2] Sir Fred Hoyle and Chandra Wickramasinghe, *Origin of Life,* (**ISBN0906449235**, imprint unknown, 1980).

befall any of us, even if the Book sternly tells that this isn't so. We may believe that we, with the Creator's blessing, are not really destroying the earth but are conducting an experiment in Government till it meets his standards—be it democracy, theocracy, communism or even tyranny.

We can believe that God is looking over our shoulder, expecting us to eventually find the right way. And then we can fantasize further about what will be next, after we have reached that blessed state. We can believe that the moon is made of green cheese and that the earth is flat and that scientists will find a solution to all of our self-inflicted woes. In fact, we can believe *anything*. There is no one to stop us, but that does not necessarily mean that we are right in doing so.

What we definitely should not do is believe without reservation anything we are *told* to believe, especially by people dressed in flowing robes, who, remarkably, all seem to have the same desire to outdo one another in wearing elaborate hats. However, no amount of gilt, glitter, expensive lace or gold leaf can be large enough to make the bringer of the message more believable than someone who shows up simply in jeans and a T-shirt.

It seems that we measure our mental capability against something we cannot fathom, and we deceive ourselves when we think that our imaginings and perceptions are superior to what we can observe.

Believing seems easy. All one has to do is say: I believe this or that. As a rule, nobody requires proof to back up what it is you believe. It may be more difficult to *un*believe things we have been made to accept as truth since childhood. Even in the face of reason we tend to cling to the popular belief systems in place all over the planet. Normally, we are not used to questioning authority. It seems indecent somehow. We are programmed to accept the status quo, and go with the flow. It is hard to acknowledge that things are not always what they seem and we are unprepared to receive and process a shock of this magnitude. Because shock is what we will experience when our belief systems change. However, we will soon discover that the new world opening up before us is not going to be detrimental to our health, physical or mental.

We have been given a brain (described by some scientists as "the most complicated structure in the universe"), which gives us the opportunity to evaluate information presented to us and to distinguish between what seems reasonable and what seems absurd. And our free will gives us the right to choose the one or the other. If we choose to prefer nonsense over logic or reason we may definitely do so, but we may not be using our unique brain to full advantage.

Belief is an intangible thing, but it certainly requires more than blind faith. Faith by itself is nothing—it needs at least a minimum of reasoning to go with it. Even faith*less*ness needs to be backed up by a certain amount of thought. It is not good enough to say: "I don't believe this or that or such and such" if the statement cannot be reinforced by some valid argument. And it is positively unnecessary to give credence to someone who tries to convince you that God appeared to him in a *dream* or as an *apparition*, and appointed him as his spokesperson, which makes him so special that from now on one must believe anything he utters. Usually at a price.

So, go believe something. But make sure it contains a reasonable amount of common sense. Not everything you hear or read is necessarily true. Not everything you hear or read is necessarily false. Use your unique brain to examine its value. You'll feel better if you do.

The Brain

Not only is the brain is the most complex organ in the body, it is also the most important part of our anatomy. It is located in the head, close to the sensory organs like eyes, ears and nose.

It is not the task of this little book to go into the physical workings of this organ. Suffice it to say that scientists have determined it contains 86 billion neurons, which constantly communicate with one another. The largest section, the cerebral cortex alone has about 30 billion neurons, connected by synapses to 10 billion more. This part controls planning, reasoning, abstract thought, self-control and probably many other aspects of being. In other words: the Mind, the Conscience, the Id. Exactly how it works is a mystery.

The brain as a whole fulfills multiple tasks: It enables us to see, hear, move, think, decide and process information. It works in many respects the same as a computer, in that it acquires information from the surrounding world, stores it, processes it in a variety of ways, so that it can be retrieved if needed, analogous to the Central Processing Unit (CPU) in a computer.

Without the brain we could not walk, talk, feel differences in temperature, recognize faces, or even eat—the normal, regular functions of living.

Moreover, the *human* brain is unique because it can be used to visualize things that do not yet exist. Most animals have brains which they use, among other things, to make nests, often very elaborate little homes, accomplished mainly by instinct, a built-in ability acquired at birth.

The human mind can see palaces, cities, spaceships, cannons, handguns, theorize how they could be made and then proceed to make them. In that way we probably are, as The God says in the Book, "made in our image." The God could be perceived as the Brain which created the universe from "nothing."

Learning

Children learn quickly and with ease. This advantage often changes when they get older. Mozart was five years old when he composed music, played the keyboard and violin. His father, Leopold, was a music teacher, but also taught the young Amadeus languages and academic subjects.

I once met a girl of four who spoke three languages fluently, knowing exactly when to speak French to her mother's friends, Dutch to her father's and English to her playmates at school. People lose that ability as they grow older—it is not easy to learn a foreign language or start piano lessons when you are, say, ninety-four.

It may be the reason why it is so difficult to *un*learn certain things that established a hold in the mind because of upbringing. The mind tends to hang on to accumulated knowledge, even if the person realizes that some of his ideas may be faulty. The brain just won't let go.

Recognition

Recognition is done by looking at people or objects and comparing the features with other items we have in our memory—a database of things we have encountered in the course of our lives. That's how we know whether we are dealing with Harry or Tom, a car or a stack of bricks.

In the abstract, we learn to distinguish between different voices, or other sounds. With our eyes closed we know who is talking, or know the difference between a car crash and a stack of bricks falling.

It is the same with information. We hear or read certain stories and we can determine whether they are worthy to be stored in our database or are better discarded since they contain expressed opinions that seem untrue or unsafe.

If we could use a parallel, the brain can be seen as our mental metabolic system, closely resembling our body's food-processing system. Information we "eat" through the ears or eyes can either benefit us our harm us. The Book exhorts us to learn the difference between good messages and bad ones. As long as we eat wholesome foods, the brain stays healthy, but if we ingest unwholesome or poisonous fare, it gets sick and may die.

Food enters the mouth and goes into the stomach, where it is broken down into smaller chunks, which go down into the long intestine. Other organs, such as the liver and the kidneys, screen and separate the wholesome from the unwholesome before it enters the rest of the system. In the long intestine, micro-organisms digest the material, and secrete a liquid that can be utilized by our body. From there the material enters the colon for final processing, separating what needs to be kept and what needs to be eliminated.

Mental metabolism

Good as well as bad information is ingested through the ears and eyes, and goes into the brain to be filtered. It stores the good with the bad for a while, until the time comes when it decides to eliminate the bad. The good information accumulates by bits and pieces until a consensus is reached, allowing the brain to become and remain healthier as we go along. By force of habit it becomes easier to distinguish between fact and fiction as the brain stores more of the good information and learns to eliminate the lies and misleading messages the world hurls at us. The Book suggests that we exercise our brain, so that it, in time, becomes an uncontaminated storehouse of solid knowledge.

The Book insinuates a future life on earth, in a new world that will last forever. That's why a clean brain may enable someone to be accepted as a citizen in this new political set-up when the time comes. It may be that this is what the Book hints at by saying that The God blew his breath into Adam's nostrils—in olden days thought to be the path to the brain. It blew away cobwebs and rats' nests, and gave Adam a clean brain when he started his mission.

Our World, dominated by Government and Religion, dishes up enormous amounts of false information, which we consume at our peril. If we keep "eating" (accepting as true) the wrong food, without eliminating it, the brain becomes poisoned (snake poison!) and we will eventually die.

Myth and tradition

There is no way to verify statements that were made many hundreds or thousands of years ago. They could be based on oral tradition, sometimes on myths and legends which may have originated way before writing was developed. The oldest written religious texts are found in Egypt and are thought to be from 2400-2300 B.C.

Many prophets have contributed their visions to the Book. The Torah, the first five books in the Book, was written in 538 B.C., after the 70-year Babylonian exile of the Jewish elite. It appears that at that time there was an outpouring of monotheistic sentiment, at least by the priesthood. It was the time that the name YHWH was brought into prominence. Many of the Minor Prophets dealt with this phenomenon. The returning priest class, eager to re-establish their own brand of power, made it appear that The God, angry at the Jews for chasing after other gods, had caused the forced exile of the elite to Babylon, leaving the remaining population in impoverished circumstances. Now some of the elite were back.

Moses, who is prominently featured in the Torah, and the person who introduced the name YHWH, was supposed to have lived about 1400 B.C., 900 years before the Torah came into existence. Nine hundred years provide ample time for oral tradition to become distorted, for myth to be added and editing to take place.

For a long time it was assumed that Moses wrote the Torah, but most scholars are now convinced that that was not the case. Ezra and Nehemiah, prophets of the post-Exile era, are the most likely authors.

Jewish religious authorities continue to expand, adapt and refine the Torah's teachings and Law to this day.

Monotheism

The Book pushes monotheism as a theme, but it is questionable whether the Jews ever practiced it before Moses came up with a name, Yahweh, for the one and only God. There is Biblical evidence that a female companion to The God existed in the land of Canaan. Her name was Asherah, also known as Ariath, Anath and Astarte. They all fell under the title, "Queen of Heaven." The Egyptian Isis was also considered such a Goddess. The prophet Jeremiah describes this "Queen of Heaven," who was revered by Hebrews living in Canaan.

In Jeremiah 7:18 he reports that Yahweh says, "The wives are kneading flour dough in order to make sacrificial cakes for the Queen of the Heavens, and there is a pouring out of drink offerings to other gods for the purpose of offending me." The prophet condemned such worship as blasphemy and a violation of the blessings of the God of Israel, and he told their husbands. But the men said they would not listen to the message. "We will burn incense to the Queen of Heaven just as we and our fathers and our officials did in the towns of Judah and in the streets of Jerusalem. At that time we had plenty of food and were well off and suffered no harm. But ever since we stopped burning incense to the Queen of Heaven and pouring out drink offerings to her, we have had nothing and have been perishing by sword and famine." (Jer. 44:15-18)

So it appears that monotheism was not necessarily a cultural tradition of the Israeli people.

The fact that Moses introduced the name Yahweh to the descendents of Abraham at the time of the alleged departure from Egypt may mean nothing more than a wish for monotheism on the insistence of the priestly class. This in turn makes it clear that the Israelis in Egypt, if they were ever there at the time, had embraced the gods of that country. The Golden Calf they built in the desert while on the way to Canaan was probably one of them.

When they arrived in Canaan, as the story suggests, they quickly adopted the gods of that region. Monotheism may have been a pipe dream of the priestly class only.

Keep all this in mind when reading or hearing about it.

The people

When scrutinizing the Torah and certainly the scriptures that follow in the Book, we begin to understand that the narration concerns every individual on the planet in those days, not just the Hebrews (or Israelites or Jews, as they were later called).

What should we make of this Book? Is it a reliable history book? For the purpose of evaluation it is of course important to know when a document of this kind was produced, and who was involved in writing it. Since it seems that the message is not directed solely at a chosen few, it might be worth exploring what it is all about.

In the first place, for a long time it was thought that the author of the Torah was Moses, but the majority of scholars have now concluded that this is not the case.

In reality, the Torah was composed, or constructed, in 538 B.C. without much distinction between myth, legend and fact. It was the legal basis for the State of Israel to function within the Persian Imperial system, which had replaced the Babylonian rule that same year. It is the *founding myth* of the Nation of Israel.

A complex and multi-layered editing process was at work. The Torah was apparently produced to settle a dispute of ownership of the land of Canaan between the wealthy landowners and the priestly class, which had just returned from exile in Babylon. The priests noticed that the Jewish nobles were oppressing the poor wherever they could.

The landowners based their ownership claim on the promise that The God had supposedly personally made to Abraham,

Isaac and Jacob, giving them and their descendents the land known as Canaan in perpetuity. The priests based it on the Moses tradition, which put the emphasis on the Exodus story and the priesthood.

Neither claim can be verified with certainty, since both relied on legend and oral tradition. No witnesses can be expected to turn up to confirm that they heard The God making such a promise to anyone. Neither can the Exodus story be said to belong in the realm of actual history because, so far, no archaeological or other evidence has turned up to corroborate whether the Exodus ever took place. Nor is there any evidence of Israelites *living* in Egypt at the time of Moses, about 1450 B.C. There is, however, a record of some Israeli settlements in Canaan during the period when Moses is said to have managed to get "his people" away from oppression by the Pharaoh of the era.

The Book says that there were two million people plus livestock departing from Egypt. The total population of Egypt around that time was 3–3.5 million. It would mean that Egypt lost more than half its population in a few days. From the foregoing it can be concluded that it is not certain that the Israelites in general were practicing a monotheistic religion.

The Exodus tradition, it should be noted, was important in the Northern Kingdom in the 8th century B.C., but not in Judea. The story appears to be of a religious rather than an historical nature—the priestly class at work, pushing Yahweh. Therefore, we needn't be alarmed if it turns out that the stories are not backed by archaeological evidence or other means of verification. The episode does point up the close relationship of Government and Religion. If the Torah was indeed written to settle a land dispute, what has it to do with Religion? It looks more as if Government, always ready to protect the wealthy, had one of its branches prepare this manuscript to protect its income base. Yet the Jews, even today, view the Torah as their holy, God-inspired book and base their religious cult ("faith") on it.

Questions come up: Where did the information the writers used come from? Were there documents predating 538 B.C.? Had Abraham's claim to the land already been established in the minds of the Jewish people? Or in the priesthood for that matter? Where does the story of Adam and Eve come from? Noah's Flood? The Exodus? Are they all myths?

It seems that the prophets Ezra and Nehemiah, who lived at the time the Torah came about, were some of the writers. They began, in Genesis, to tell what their God had accomplished.

The God

Many creation stories exist, many from antiquity, and each culture seems to have its own, but here is the Book's account:

Right from the start, in Genesis, it tells us that there is a God and that he created the heavens, the earth and everything else, including us. He makes it known in the opening chapters that he exists "in the heavens" and that he created—or caused to be created—the entire universe with its billions of stars, galaxies, nebulae and planets, our Earth being one of them.

Our planet is singled out in the narrative. Extensive coverage is spent on its flora and fauna, including us. No particulars are given as to how many other planets may have the same characteristics and are also enjoying life as we know it. Some speculate that it could hardly be possible for other "worlds" to not exist, given the billions and billions of stars, planets and galaxies in the universe, but that's what it is: speculation. The Book does not enlighten us. There are, however, thousands of books suggesting that it is so, even offering descriptions of such a "world," its inhabitants and their lifestyle. Whether or not they are more believable than the Book is for the reader to decide.

Because of the claim that The God created our planet with all its appurtenances, he also lets us know that, apart from being its Creator, he is also its Owner, consequently its legitimate Ruler, entitled to retaliate when his right to rule is challenged.

Opposition is not allowed, nor is it, as it turns out, good for the opposing party, who will certainly be punished, standing the chance of elimination from the scene altogether.

Opposition

An important part of the Book deals with a takeover that happened six thousand or more years ago, as described in the first chapters of Genesis. It alerts us to the existence of an illegal and oppressive World Government, ruled by its own anonymous god, who pretends to be the Almighty. He is the god admired and worshipped by the World. The story of Adam and Eve is in essence the story of the start of that illegitimate, inept regime.

It is made clear in everything that follows that the resulting World, with its various nations, is not a setup favored by The God. Throughout the Book he promises to make drastic and dramatic changes in the near future. From the very beginnings of the takeover he vowed to install his own Government: a "Kingdom of the Heavens," which, apparently, was the original idea. A Kingdom that will be for ever and ever. *Heavens,* as used here, is a metaphor for excellence, perfection. Those professing a wish to be included in it can say so and will get a chance to become its citizens. The message implies that they will have "life eternal" as Adam and Eve had before they "fell."

Those who choose not to be included and would rather stay with the world as it is can also say so and consequently run the risk of annihilation, or destruction of their person, or "soul," in the coming world. "Soul" is not limited to humans—even animals are identified as souls (living, breathing beings) in the writings. Nowhere in The Book is there any mention of people *having* souls; it is clear that a soul is treated as a living unit, and that a soul can, and will, also die (Ezekiel 18:4).

The choices are made plain, in order to avoid confusion as to what is what and who is who. The Book acknowledges that there are many gods (1 Cor. 8:5), but only one Supreme Being, who wishes to be recognized as the one and only real God, above all other gods, and known by his name, YHWH.

The Book also makes it clear that The God works on a different time scale than we humans. Creation days are counted in millions and millions of years, which makes a thousand years a fleeting moment. Therefore it may be folly to believe that he will not keep his word if he says that he will make changes. It may seem to us that it will never happen, because the World continues on its violent path seemingly forever, but a few hundred years here or there do not mean much in Yahweh's time scale. For those individuals who believe in this prediction, and are willing to forego the "pleasures" of the World, it means patience.

Those who are "chosen" in this manner, citizens of the new Kingdom, are sometimes called *Israelites*, or *his people*, or *the holy ones*. Holy means special (Deut. 7:6), and chosen does not mean randomly picked and made holy in an instant. In order to qualify, one must have a complete change of mind about our world setup and be open to what the new system will be like and accept the challenges brought about by one's decision.

It is clear that the epithet "Israel" is a metaphor for a people looked upon with favor by The God, and it does not matter what nationality a possible member goes by in the present World. It is extremely doubtful that the modern country of Israel, now being one of the "nations" detested by The God, could be that nation.

The World's rulers are not eager to hear this message of the end of the world and the installation of a heavenly Government. It would mean the end of the good times for them. Their preferred treatment of the subject is ridicule. It is often difficult for those who do believe in it to cope with the negative attitude and ostracism coming to them from airing their point of view.

The Book also tells us that Religion, as the world practices it, is fake (Luke 20:46-47). It becomes evident that it was originally made up by Government to cover up its inability to govern. Its dogmas are carefully maintained because of the many perks it presents to the present system's rulers. Not many people realize that Organized Religion is the foundation upon which the system rests, and that it would collapse if its dogmas were to be disbelieved by an overwhelming majority of people.

How Holy the Spirit

Few words in the Book have been so badly misunderstood by the majority of its readers as the word "spirit." At times, mainly because of the machinations of Religion, it was synonymous with "ghost," as in "Holy Ghost," or with a transparent body. "Spirits" coming through in séances were believed to be the souls of the departed seeking to communicate with their loves ones still on earth. They were understood to be housed in a realm somewhere in space, waiting to be summoned (often for a fee) by the person who knew how to get in touch with them.

However...

Nowhere in the Book does it state that a spirit is a person, and certainly not the soul of a dead person. In this book about the Book, the word "spirit" should be understood as "in the spirit of."

In this sense, "spirit" is a way of thinking, or a way of doing things. A person could do, say or think something in the spirit of the time, in the spirit of goodwill, in the spirit of motherhood, in the spirit of Shakespeare, or whatever. In this way we could also see the connection with "Holy Spirit," which, in essence, is a special way of looking at the world around us, and how we think about it.

The word *holy* has become a word almost exclusively claimed by Bible thumpers as a synonym for *purity*, and *without sin*, as if it only pertained to people dressed in white robes, swinging a Bible in front of those who they consider impure and aim to make as holy as themselves.

As the World understands it, a *Pope* is supposed to be Holy. Some *priests* are thought to be. An occasional *nun* may get the epithet, Mother Teresa being one of them. It seems hard to compete with their ilk. But is being Holy such an unreachable goal? What *does* "Holy" really mean?

The Book treats the word "holy" as if it were synonymous with "special," or "different," or "set apart" (Deut. 7:6-7).

Most people, observing the World, see an ongoing experiment of Governments striving to provide their subjects with a good life, ever getting better at it. The occasional war, with the misery it brings, is seen as a necessary part of this ongoing experiment—a passing phase soon to be done away with, in a combined effort.

Organized Religion, being very much a part of that violent world, is viewed as a multi-faceted institution helping the population and their governments to eventually reach the Utopian goal of Peace on earth, assisted by an unseen, benign, ever-loving, ever-forgiving Being: their God. Religions therefore, regardless of denomination, are recognized by Governments in most of the world as beneficial and helpful organizations; certainly not as enemies of their State.

There are other individuals, however, who do not go along with this view at all. They look at the same World and see a bombastic try at Government; a flawed, corrupt, violent system of individual, competing nations, constantly warring with one another, a system definitely not run by a benign, ever-loving Being, but rather by a dark Force *calling* itself God, erroneously believed by the majority of the world's population to be the original Creator of the universe. They observe its obnoxious military might, its greed, its violent rhetoric, its disregard for the laws of nature, and it goes without saying that they would welcome a change. They also agree that the dark Force behind it is the father of Organized Religion, the institution he uses to hide the truth about his World as long as possible.

However, using their brain would also tell them before long that reversing the combined thinking of the World, the World's

Spirit, is such a formidable task that it cannot be accomplished by mere mortals. Jesus thought about it and decided he could not do it while he was on earth "in the flesh."

The brain may tell you that joining an army and going into battle will never produce the peaceful earth promised by Governments. Or that, although cutting down a forest could be expected to produce a temporary boost to some country's economy, and improved goodwill for its rulers, it could also be seen an example of the rulers' shortsightedness, because floods, landslides and maybe other disasters are usually produced downstream.

The people with such a spirit *are* therefore "special," "different," "set apart" from the world, or "holy" (Deut. 7:6-7). They have a sense of having been set free; almost as if they had become citizens of a different "nation," living in the midst of an oppressive world, somewhat similar to the story of the people of ancient Israel being in bondage in Egypt longing for their freedom.

And that is what "Holy Spirit" means.

No more, no less.

This conclusion does not sit well with either the various Governments or the many branches of Religion, all going out of their way to ridicule those who have come to this realization, all trying to stop efforts to broadcast such an unwelcome message.

However, once a person has come to see the truth about the World, it becomes very difficult not to talk about it with "neighbors." Not necessarily in an effort to *convert* them, but to convince *themselves* by listening to the others' answers and opinions that their *own* view is correct.

Such a person will show you many instances in the Book where it points to the "End of the World," which they see with great joy and conviction to be the end of the flawed system, including the demise of the world's fake Religions.

Organized Religion cannot successfully deny that this information exists, but has, with the help of more than willing

Governments, managed to change the meaning of "End of the World" to "End of the Planet," insinuating that God will blow his beautiful creation, with us on it, to bits. The most surprising thing is that the Book is the very book claimed by Organized Religion as the basis for its own dogmas.

"Planet" and "World"

We can look at the planet and its workings. It is tangible, it can be touched. We can eat the food the soil provides and stay healthy. We can use the various minerals in the soil to make things. We can build structures on the planet, of wood, stone, or clay and to a certain extent change the nature of the minerals we use. However, we also find that when we do, our actions have an effect on nature. The effect becomes more intense with the increase in population, since more and more people need the same supply of resources, which are not unlimited. That we cannot change. What you see is what you get.

The World and its workings can only be described. We can point to our institutions such as Government, Religion and the Monetary system, point to the effect they have on our lives and judge whether we are happy with the way the World works or not. If we don't like it, we may be able to do something about it, but our chances to do so are limited.

Civilization, apparently, has some unwelcome characteristics, like violence. Stopping it seems impossible. We can vote and protest and hope for a result. We can ignore the World altogether. However, escape is not an option—living in the World is part of living on the planet. We have to deal with the mechanics of it whether we like it or not.

For most of pre-history people lived in stateless societies, a state being an organized community living under one government. The first known state came into existence approximately 5,500 years ago, established by the Sumerians, who introduced writing, mathematics, astronomy, astrology, written law, agriculture, architecture, organized medicine and wheeled vehicles.

The Book provides a record of the coup that took place six thousand years ago and differentiates between what The God deems legal or illegal. In its many pages it describes the present style of Government, how it came into existence and how it will be dealt with by Yahweh. This is not presented as one simple statement—the information often comes in the form of a hint, a pointer alerting the reader that illegality and change is discussed. A good example is the dream of king Nebuchadnezzar (Daniel 2: 31-45), where the one after the other world government is dealt with as parts of a large statue, diminishing in quality as time goes by, from the golden head to the feet of clay, and its eventual destruction by a pebble.

A promise

From Genesis to Revelations the theme is the same: the promise that Yahweh is going to bring down the present world and start anew with a totally different outlook. The reader must decide if this contains truth and whether to go with the one or the other.

It is practically impossible to discuss Government and civilization on the planet without mentioning Organized Religion. They are so closely related that is often difficult to separate the two. Our civilization hinges on the way we are being governed and the way we think about gods and death and dying. That is where Religion comes in.

As a general rule one could look at a particular Religion and see if it is condoned or encouraged by Government. If it is condoned, it's imitation; if it is not, it is probably painfully close to the truth.

The snake that talked

The talking snake has been an object of ridicule over the years. It has been the butt of jokes by some television talk show hosts. "A talking snake? Come on! Grow up! This Book is such a ludicrous bunch of nonsense; it is not worth our attention in this modern age!"

There is something to be said for that. Snakes don't talk. Snakes never, ever talked. Neither did any other beasts or reptiles of the field ever open their mouths or beaks for any other purpose than eating, catching prey, peeping, barking or growling. It is preposterous to assume they ever did communicate with human beings by using actual language.

Strange punishment

The situation gets worse when later on we read about parts of the punishment which The God metes out for the snake: "From now on you will crawl on your belly and eat dust."

Since we know what a snake looks like it seems a puzzling, unnecessary punishment. As far as we know, snakes have always crawled on their bellies in the dust of the earth and were therefore prone to get dust in their food. Unless, of course, this particular snake had legs before he convinced the woman to partake of the forbidden fruit. Also an impossible and ridiculous assumption.

The Fruits of Eden, this book about the Book, is written to address the snake business as well as the fruit business and many other puzzling topics. Who is Yahweh? Who was Moses, who explained who Yahweh was? Who is Satan? What is Religion? Are Jews different from the rest of the population? Why do we die? And what then?

It will all be "apocalypsed," in this book, in due course.

Eve Ate: A short history of *un*civilization

Going back to the beginning of the Book, to the Garden of Eden story, we encounter the snake talking a woman into eating a certain fruit. As we read further we may conclude that "eating," "talking," "hearing" and "seeing," in this instance, may not be functions of the body but functions of the mind.

It is apparent that the Book is not a novel, and if you are trying to read it like one, you will soon be confused and frustrated. It does contain stories, but they do not necessarily have a *historical* significance. Symbolism of one kind or another is used throughout the Book. Whatever it is conveying is spread throughout its hundreds of pages, often in snippets of information, which, when combined like a jigsaw puzzle, lead to the message. It describes the beginning of "the World"—the unsatisfactory system under which we live—and promises an end to it.

The core message is that Yahweh, the God, who made everything that exists, is also its legitimate ruler, and that anyone who cuts in and takes over that prerogative is doomed to failure and death. This theme recurs throughout its many pages, making the Book a political manifesto rather than a morality manual. It is also imperative to recognize that the message is often given in the form of parables, the meaning of which needs to be analyzed to be properly understood. As a political manifesto, the message does not reflect favorably upon the present World, and its variety of diverse governments. That's why those who run the World do not want this information to become public knowledge, and use various methods to counteract it.

Creation: Beginning

Each culture has its own creation story, many from antiquity, but here is what the Book says:

God created the heavens, the earth and everything else, including us. His creative activity was measured in "days." These were not 24-hour days. Considering that the age of the earth is estimated at 4.5 billion years (possibly more), and that there are 7 days involved, including his rest day, we see that one day was at least 600 million years long, if we assume that a day was $1/7^{th}$ of 4.5 billion. The "days" were symbols for such a period of time.

The earth was still without form, and there was "darkness upon the surface of the watery deep." Then he said: "Let light come to be." This was not our sun. The sun came later. The light referred to must have been of the symbolic kind.

It may have been the creation of one of what the Book calls "angels," this one a spirit named Lucifer, who originally was an "angel of Light," in charge of making sure that Yahweh's plans for the planet were carried out. God made a difference between a condition of Light and a condition of Darkness, or the difference between good and bad. He began to call the light *Day* and the darkness *Night*.

On the second day God created the expanse, and a division between the waters beneath the expanse and the waters above the expanse. He began to call the expanse *Heaven*.

On the third day he made dry land appear. He called the dry land *earth*, and the collection of waters *Seas*. He made grasses appear, and vegetation bearing fruit.

On the fourth day he created the sun and the moon and also the stars in the expanse of the heavens, to serve as signs for seasons and for days and years.

On the fifth day he made the waters swarm with living souls and the air with flying creatures. He blessed them and told them to be fruitful and become many.

The sixth and seventh days are exceptional. If we do not understand what happened on the sixth day, then what happened on the seventh day makes no sense at all.

On the sixth day God let the earth put forth living souls, domestic animal and wild beast and every creeping animal according to its kind. And he saw that it was good. After that he made man *"in our image, according to our likeness"* and let them have dominion over the entire animal world. *Male and female he created them.*

He blessed them and told them to be fruitful and fill the earth. Vegetation was to be the food of man and animal.

On the seventh day God rested from all his works. In Gen 2:5, however, we read that as yet there was no shrub or vegetation found in the earth, because The God had not made it rain yet; neither was there a "Man" to cultivate the ground, regardless of what passed on day six. The ground was watered by a vapor that went up continually to water the entire surface. This seeming discrepancy may exist because this information, too, may be symbolic, as noted above.

The Man

Then God formed the Man out of dust, or clay, and blew into his nostrils the *breath of life*, whereby the Man became a living soul, a breathing person. This breath of life is not mentioned on day six, when God made man, male and female. Neither does it state that in this later instance he created *male and female*, but "the Man" by himself. *Therefore, it is reasonable to conclude that the male and female mentioned in day six are not the same as the man who later became known as Adam.* This conclusion is validated by DNA research that has proven that human beings were on earth tens of thousands of years before Adam, who was created only about six thousand years ago, according to the Book's chronology.

If we recognize the time frame in which God operates we will understand that creating a living being was not done in an afternoon. The man was made of the dust of the earth (DNA?), so it is possible that he was born the normal way and then separated from the rest of the indigenous population to be educated in the ways of Yahweh, by blowing "the breath of life" into his nostrils. He was a special, or holy, creation, most likely to be groomed to become the planet's King of the Kingdom of the Heavens. That required learning time.

God planted a garden for the Man, with many trees bearing fruit, good to eat. There was a *tree of life* in the middle of the garden and also the *tree of the knowledge of good and evil*. The Man could eat the fruit from all of the trees freely. Symbol after symbol—the word *eating* is often used in the Bible as a synonym for consuming knowledge, or learning. The "rain" mentioned earlier represented the learning process, and the missing "Man" represented the fact that there was as yet nobody to teach the indigenous people about Yahweh's plan for the planet. However, he was not allowed to eat the fruit of the good and evil tree. This was not just a test to see if the Man would be strong enough to resist eating, say, a banana, even if it looked innocuous and smelled appetizing. There was a different and very valuable reason for that command, if we take into consideration what followed.

The Garden of Eden was not a real garden, and neither of these trees were actual trees. The trees were symbols for areas of learning, and all the trees most likely had names like knowledge of the earth (and its workings), knowledge of the flora and fauna, knowledge of the oceans and rivers, knowledge of nature in general, knowledge of other planets, the universe, knowledge of everything: *God's university*. The "breath of life," may have been a metaphor for the learning process, since knowledge is necessary for a healthy brain, and a healthy brain is necessary for survival.

The foregoing explains why the location of the Garden of Eden has never been found. It never existed as an orchard. God's University could have been anywhere on the planet. Learning is not bound to any geographical area—it can be done in a ship at sea for that matter.

The "breath of life into his nostrils" made it also possible for the pupil to understand that he was special, and that he should not get involved with the existing population until much later, when he was finished with his studies.

The Man could not have avoided noticing that the primitive tribes had a tendency for roughness and violence, presenting the possibility that he would be contaminated with that behavior before he knew how to recognize good from evil.

In other words, he would then learn that there *was* a difference before he had acquired sufficient knowledge to deal with it properly.

If he did choose to become involved, his brain would become compromised, contaminated with their ways, and that would be the end of his right to life in the Kingdom. In the day he *did* stray he would *most certainly* die. This is stated without any extenuating circumstances, as for example: not *really* dying if certain conditions were met, so that some part of him could keep on living some other way, or somewhere else.

A person lives as long as his brain is alive. Kill the brain and the person dies. The brain acts as if it were a radio or television receiver that can be tuned to any station or channel to receive information, be it good or bad. It is likely that a person could live "forever" as long as his brain remained pure, uncontaminated.

The pure brain of the Man, later called Adam, was the result of the education he received, which did not involve impurity of thought. We learn later, in other snippets of information, that Lucifer, the angel of Light, was appointed by The God to see to it that Adam did not stray from this perfect situation. Exactly how this was done is not clear. Inspiration by telepathy seems a likely scenario.

However, any brain is also capable of receiving bad information, and a person is free to do so. He or she must then determine which information is good or bad, and act on it. Or, if he/she was not yet capable of discernment, obey a certain command. Acting on suggestions to do the wrong thing *poisons the brain.* And this kind of (snake) poison kills the person as well, maybe not immediately, but certainly in due time. The Book reports that Adam, who did act upon the wrong information, was 930 years old when he died, but die he did. It does not say that his soul went places after he passed away. It simply states that he died, period.

Although Adam supposedly died when he was 930 years old, technically he was dead from the day he "ate" (1 Cor. 15:22). The parallel with the fruit of the forbidden tree in the Garden of Eden and the serpent lying about the consequences of eating it is clear: The God had said, "If you eat of this tree, you will most certainly die." However, to this day Organized Religion will tell you that the serpent (Satan) was right. Our body may die, but the "soul" lives on, in heaven, with God.

Eve

The story of how the woman, later called Eve, came into existence most likely had mythical origins. The deep sleep and the rib taken from Adam to form the female are events that are not easily understood, but that is the information the Book gives us. She became a part of him, "one flesh." It may also have been meant symbolically, but it is not easy to say in what way.

She, too, was a living soul, and could therefore also "communicate" with the Deity. However, like anyone, she could listen to a different radio station and either accept or reject the suggestions presented. The Book reports that she was also aware of the warning not to eat from the tree of knowledge of good and bad, at least not yet.

If the Book's chronology is correct, the couple lived about six thousand years ago, in Mesopotamia, "the Land between the rivers." That is the archaeological episode known as the Ubaid Period, from 5300-4700 B.C.

Eve's compassionate spirit

It is more than likely that Eve had superior knowledge about the earth and nature because she also attended God's University. She must have been familiar with the fact that agriculture on a small, personal scale had been in use for thousands of years, with no discernible damage to the environment. However, as she observed the various nomadic tribes who for tens of thousands of years had been traveling from place to place in their quest for sustenance, she probably developed the idea of teaching them how to use grain modification and irrigation techniques to grow food on a large scale, so that they could stop being nomadic. She may also have thought that recourse to plenty of food would civilize them and curb their violent habits which were often caused by the occasional scarcity of food.

The idea was very attractive and she decided to implement it. When she told Adam about her plan, he reminded her that dealing with the primitive population constituted eating from the forbidden tree, warning her that she would most certainly die if she continued on that path. At first he declined to assist Eve with her plan.

In the Book's account, symbols are used, reporting that a "serpent" spoke to Eve, convincing her that they positively would not die if they "ate" the forbidden fruit. They would become like gods instead, knowing good and evil. In further information we learn that the serpent was Lucifer, who later became known as the Great Deceiver, or Satan, the Devil. The concept of Satan, therefore, constitutes *our own inclination* to be self-important, arrogant, conceited, thinking we can succeed without "heavenly," or pure input. By Eve's actions our world came to be ruled by "Satan," our own arrogant inclinations.

Eve ignored Adam's warning and went ahead. Agriculture on a big scale was introduced. Marshes were drained, canals dug, irrigation programs implemented.

It soon became clear that monoculture creates the necessity to stay in one place, because you cannot very well leave large fields of growth unattended for any length of time. It meant that houses had to be built.

Because of nature's abundance, surpluses became an issue after harvest time, and a need for granaries and other storehouses arose. A central government was established to oversee the work that needed to be done. Later, writing and a system of bookkeeping had to be developed to keep track of the status of the storehouses.

When Adam saw that Eve did not die on the spot, as he had feared, he agreed to help her. Both may even have come to the conclusion that they had not interpreted the information about the good and bad tree correctly.

What was so bad about what Eve was doing? It worked! And if it worked on this relatively small scale, it could be expanded to include the rest of the planet! The wish for world domination was born. A greed-based, opportunistic management idea.

However, where Eve's prime involvement was of the female variety—motherly, protective and caring—a sentiment probably initially shared by Adam, his cooperation eventually became something else. Adam had observed the behavior of the tribal chiefs of the indigenous population, who had concluded that, without manipulation and exploitation it was not possible to protect their tribe from the aggression of other tribes. He soon began to copy their policies. Strong-arm tactics were needed to protect Adam and Eve's new cities and storehouses. A standing army became a necessity.

Because of their "eternal" status, it must have appeared to the pair that the commoners, whose lifespan came to about forty years, but kept reproducing while alive, were a continuous source of labor and soldiers: a never-ending but expendable resource. Producing babies became a protected activity.

The Fruits of Eden were inexorably introducing themselves, but it took some time to realize it.

Adam's cooperation resulted in the establishment of the world we see around us. At first an elite class of hereditary chieftains came into being. They, their descendents and often cronies, became the eventual rulers of hundreds of "sovereign" nations, each with its own rules and laws, often warring with one another, damaging the environment and causing climate change, of which we have not seen the end yet today.

The start of our World

Adam, Eve, their children and grandchildren became the first leaders of the then known world. No wonder they thought of themselves as gods, a way of thinking that permeated the behavior of subsequent leaders. It displays an arrogant spirit, a feeling of center-of-the-world importance.

Genetically Modified Organisms (GMOs), one of the later fruits of Eden

What they could not have foreseen was that someone, or some group or organization, would eventually succeed to *industrialize* agriculture, on an immensely larger scale, producing genetically modified foods, some with built-in pesticides, jeopardizing the health of its customers, profit being the sole objective for its activities. Some items of vegetation, once modified, would even become objects for patenting, thereby monopolizing the production of that particular food and threatening or even eliminating the competition. Here, too, the goal is world domination, fueled by money generated by greed.

(Accumulation of wealth for a small elite part of the population is still an integral part of the world domination syndrome. Wealth constitutes power. The wealthier one is, the easier the way to power becomes. It seems that today one cannot become a world leader without spending untold millions, either one's own funds or those supplied by other persons or organizations intent on world domination, politically, economically, religiously, or otherwise.)

The area of Mesopotamia where this took place is generally called the "Cradle of Civilization." If we consider the results of the actions taken by the pair in that time period, a more accurate description would be the "cradle of greed, inept world domination and manipulated myth"—high finance, politics and fake religion. Or, in other words, *un*civilization. Not everyone is likely to agree with this statement, but we will come back to it later with an explanation.

Adam and Eve, innocent of what they had started, began to think that Yahweh had been wrong in keeping them away from this very successful and lucrative enterprise. They may have thought they created the perfect world. Eventually they immured themselves against any thought of the Almighty, eliminated every reference to Yahweh from their conscience, and began to support the superstitious ideas that the locals had about nature. Hence: Fake Religion.

True and false religious thinking

True religion is different. What we know about it has come to us from prophets. A prophet will indicate what, in his (and Yahweh's) opinion, is the difference between real and false, or fake, religion.

Prophets determined and declared that the only *true* religion is the recognition that Yahweh exists, and the expressed appreciation of what he has done: create a perfect earth for us, with its abundance of flora and fauna, and with everything connected to it that contributes to the pleasure of living. What we have *done* to the planet makes it less attractive, but they considered that not Yahweh's fault.

If appreciation for the planet and its workings is *true* religion, it follows that *false* religion is the opposite: the expectation of something better later on.

Hoping to be removed from our planet to a much better place shows disrespect and is an affront to Yahweh. The very idea of such an afterlife, either in "heaven" or anywhere else shows misunderstanding of Yahweh's plan for his planet. He has no use for people who think along those lines, calls them godless, "wicked" and indicates that he will delete them from his Scroll (book) of Life (Psalm 37:20, 1 Sam 2:6, Rev 14:10-13).

A prophet recognizes that *bad conditions* on the planet are man-made. However, the present man-made situation leads some people to believe that other "worlds" exist where conditions are "more advanced," which make them desirous to leave. Again others believe that the citizenry of one of those much more civilized "worlds" will come to our planet and teach us a thing or two about behavior in the universe. It is the kind of scornful attitude that is loathed by Yahweh, who has announced that he will reverse the trend of our ignorant and destructive ways when he installs his own government, after the interruption caused by Adam and Eve, which is still going on.

This is not to be seen as an improvement to the planet's *workings*, which, The God said, were "very good" from the beginning. He did say, however, that he would restore it to its original perfect condition.

Many fake religious cults abide throughout the world, two of them prominent, all based on the same lies and fantastic afterlife scenarios, all in cahoots with big government, making sure that the population at large does not find out why the World is the way it is.

Taking the Name in vain

Mentioning the name "Yahweh" is still considered taboo by Religion. It is either thought to be equal to taking the Lord's name in vain by cussing, or, as in the Jewish "Faith" (Is there something called "a faith"?), where uttering the name is superstitiously seen as forbidden by Elohim (God). Again others regard it as bad luck. These days, especially since the appearance of sects using the name in one form or another, (*Jehovah's* Witnesses), the Name is treated with derision, as are the Witnesses themselves. Anyone who uses the name Yahweh or Jehovah is deemed by Organized Religion to be a silly zealot.

It has been impressed upon people that it is not important whether God has a proper name or not, although they themselves would not be satisfied to be called "carpenter" or "blacksmith," or "bookkeeper." Making The God anonymous is not accidental. Making the Name disappear was a conscious act to hide the knowledge that we are not really governed by the Creator, but by our own highly respected arrogance and ignorance. It is a disguised ploy to cover-up the fact that his intended peaceful government was hijacked by greed, power hunger and black magic.

The goal is to make people unaware that The God exists, that he is unique, and that he has a name. He wants the name to be known, the prophets say, because without it he cannot be distinguished from other gods, like "the Lord," or simply "God." The anonymous epithet "God" or "Lord" is what is used in most Bibles to describe the godhead, and practically everyone equates it with the Creator, and that suits the World's leaders fine. However, in the Book, the "Our Father" prayer begins with "your *name* be sanctified" (Matthew 6:9-13), implying that, so far, it has not been.

Again, if the Book's premise can be believed, and Sin is deadly, it means that Sin is our *group activity*, instigated and led by our religious and secular leaders and by default condoned by us.

Cain and Abel

The symbolism behind the story of Cain and Abel is not well understood by the majority of people. It depicts the divisions in the World and explains why Cain will be avenged seven times.

The Book does not supply us with the ages of the two brothers, but we can assume that they were grown men when Cain murdered Abel. When we consider that the trespass of Eve and Adam happened within 130 years after Adam's beginning, with the birth of Seth, it seems reasonable to assume that Eve thought that Abel (a Man) was the promised "seed," who would turn the world back to its pristine beginnings and give them back their right to life in the Kingdom.

Cain, on the other hand, did not qualify for that role, because he became a "tiller of the ground," which probably meant that he was in charge of the large-scale agricultural activity. It is not likely that he would be mentioned in a Book such as this had he merely become a farmer. He may have been involved with the invention and application of the plough.

The role of a herder

Abel, however, did not participate in the developing World. He was clearly a voice for Yahweh and represented the opposition. He was a "sheepherder," a title rather than a profession. Had he been a literal sheepherder, he would not have deserved mention either. It meant that he was the leader of a group or tribe. The group was his following in his quest to warn (preach) of the dangerous path the world was taking.

When Cain killed Abel, Cain feared that anyone finding him would certainly kill him, almost certainly pointing to Abel's followers. But The God soon made it clear that the World would exonerate Cain (seven times!) and actually thank him for eliminating the nuisance factor.

Organized Religion, interpreting the Book literally, wants us to believe that Adam, Eve, Cain and Abel were then the only four people on earth. If this were so, who would be the "anyone finding him"? His parents?

The promise of a redeemer had already been given, as is apparent in the murder story. It also means that Adam and Eve's trespass had been going on while Cain and Abel were growing up. The *animal offering* conducted by Abel was a reminder that someone would appear who would successfully withstand satanic thoughts and actions, and be killed as a sacrificial lamb for speaking out against the establishment.

Seen in this light it appears that not only a person like Abel, but anyone arguing against the System runs the risk of being eliminated one way or another.

Adam and Eve—Realization 1

To resume the narrative of Adam and Eve: It did not take long for them to realize that they had made a huge mistake. Within 130 years it became apparent that they were not adequately equipped to deal with the developing situation. However, by that time their children and grandchildren were heavily involved in running the scheme, which made it practically impossible to turn back and undo it. The Bible calls this "inherited sin."

In the course of time it probably dawned on the couple that some enterprising person—even one of their own children or grandchildren—could very well push them aside and take over this lucrative empire, if necessary by force. To discourage such a violent takeover the fairy tale was originated that people *have* souls, and that good people's souls *(read: people not posing a threat to the government)* at the moment of their death went to a wonderful place called Heaven, where they would meet God himself. Bad people *(read: those posing a threat to the government)* went to a terrible place called Hell, where they would be tortured forever by a person called Satan the Devil. This may have discouraged some aspiring leaders, but not everyone became a believer in the fabrications. Takeovers happened anyway. The blatant lies, however, are still the basis of Organized Religion, with the continued blessing of Government.

It deserves mention that there is a definite relationship with modern "Christianity" and Babylon when we consider the language angle. The language for daily use in Babylon was *Akkadian*, but the language used in religious services was *Sumerian*, which was by then a dead language. The similarity with the Latin language used by the Catholic religion is striking. It gave and still gives the clergy every opportunity to misuse power by obscuring truth, to obfuscate, lie and confuse.

Adam and Eve—Realization 2: The naked truth

After Adam and Eve had come to the conclusion that they did not have the required knowledge to be the world's rulers (Genesis 3:7, "their eyes were opened"), they tried to "hide." Yahweh found them in the garden, covered with fig leaves they had sewn together because they were "naked." Fig leaves are a metaphor for shame, and the nakedness symbolized their lack of knowledge necessary to run the world properly.

The idea that weaving and the manufacture of clothes was unknown and that our pair always walked around naked is a religious fallacy.

It is interesting to read that they were "in the garden" when Yahweh found them. They had gone back to the University, whose instructions they had ignored, to find answers to the dilemma they had created. They were in deep trouble and returned to see if the University provided an answer to the pressing question: how to tell your charges you have made a serious mistake? How to ask thousands of people to abandon the new lifestyle, stop large-scale agriculture, leave their cities and become nomads again?

The University offered no solutions to their problem. Lucifer, if we see him as an individual, could not help out, because he didn't know what to do about it either. It was *his* world after all, and he may have thought that everything would come out all right in the end. Symbolically "thrown out of heaven," he had been cut off from further useful knowledge. Adam and Eve were now left to their own devices. Here they were, with their flimsy fig leaf covering, symbolically standing in front of the angel with the flaming sword, who guarded the closed doors of the University.

When God "spoke" to them and asked them what they had done Eve blamed the Serpent, who had deceived her, Adam blamed The God, because he had given him Eve, who had deceived him (Gen 3:10, etc.). God then cursed the serpent, telling him he would "crawl on his belly and eat dust," and that he would put enmity between him and the *woman*[3] and his seed and her seed,[4] meaning that one of her "seeds" (offspring) would become a redeemer, a replacement for Adam, another living soul, qualified to start anew (Genesis 3:14-15).

Civilization or *un*civilization

The word "civilization" has most likely been coined by a government worker, a member of the Establishment—or, even more likely, by a member of the *Religious branch* of the Establishment. The epithet implies that we are a civilized bunch—nice God-fearing people, good people, excellent people, who would not willingly hurt other, equally good, nice people. In the main, this is a true statement. If it were it not for the influence of the powers-that-be, the planet's population would be relatively peaceful.

Because . . .

Violence is the hallmark of our civilization. And that is not very civil. History consists almost exclusively of reports of wars conducted by various kings and other government persons, sometimes even religious leaders. Consider this: leaders of the past were often judged favorably by the amount of violence they

---

[3] The woman introduced here is not Eve per se. "She" constitutes the opposition to Satan and his world. Here a distinction is made between a faithful Woman, who dispenses wholesome "food" to her children (Matthew 24:45), correct information supplied by the "Father," and the unfaithful Woman, Organized Religion (the Whore of Babylon in Revelations) who supplies her children with unwholesome food or false, conflicting information, gleaned from the many sources she is beholden to. (See all of Revelations 17.)

[4] In the King James translation, the article of the seed is "it," pointing to a situation rather than an actual person—"something" rather than "someone."Her seed against that of the serpent would indicate that a future situation is meant. Her seed would be truth, his would be falsehood. Truth would prevail. The so-far-unnamed woman is now given the name Eve "because she had to become the mother of everyone living," or "no longer dying," those free from the Adamic death curse, Yahweh's "Israelites," living citizens of his Kingdom.

had at their disposal to defeat and conquer an "enemy." The level of violence often determined which leader was deemed worthy to be called "great" in our history books. Civilization indeed! It is not a pretty picture.

But what about Religion? Doesn't that show that we are peaceful? We go to our various churches and often pray for peace, don't we? We even confess that we are appalled by the forty or so wars going on all over the planet day after day. We may be convinced that God is testing us to see how much of it we can stand before our leaders find the perfect solution.

However, a legitimate question is: what has Religion ever done about it? It has a very disappointing record in that respect. One of the functions of Religion is to manipulate the world's population into *accepting* violence as a means to an end. Think of the way fallen soldiers are glorified, hailed as heroes and martyrs for God's good cause, sprinkling holy water on their caskets. This treatment keeps people in awe of Religion and enables Governments to practice violence and destruction to the full; violence sanctified for their mutual benefit and survival.

There are those who cynically refer to Government and Religion as two peas in a pod, but even that is faulty reasoning. They are one pea in one pod. No matter how often they try to convince us that separation of Church and State exists, it doesn't. It is one of the lies we have been taught to accept as truth. Religion, in effect, is a *branch* of Government, the same way the army, the police, the justice system, education, and other services are branches. The connection may not be obvious, but it is there. The one could not really survive without the other.

Why does Religion exist in the first place?

The religious branch is a *necessity* for Government. It was created to intimidate, manipulate and misinform. If you want to give a war, for example, Religion is one of the better tools to convince your population that some other population is an enemy, and certainly if the perceived enemy's Religion is different from yours. Any amount of questionable information can be used. Outright lies, repeated and repeated, eventually get an aura of respectability if they are uttered by people in high places. High places are high because they tell us they are.

Once the enemy threat has been established, the next step is to convince your population of the necessity to kill some of the other population, or at least destroy their property. The priest sanctified the action, taking away the possible doubts or misgivings of the population and almost certainly blessed the soldiers in the name of whatever God. This enabled the leader to annex or dominate some or all of the enemy's real estate, thereby its wealth, and consequently increase his or her power.

The world's original leaders were often proclaimed to *be* God, or at least his offspring, and used Organized Religion to protect that image. Religious functionaries, most likely trusted family members in those ancient days, applied incantations and paraphernalia to imprint on the common folk the divine connection the present ruler had with God. It was made clear that God would punish those who dared interfere with the Ruler's mission to do God's will.

Intimidation of this kind, the fear of retaliation from the Deity, prevented the average subject from trying to take over the absolute (and very lucrative) power of the King. Without the backing and maybe the assistance of the religious establishment a coup was practically impossible.

However, it sometimes happened that the vigilance became a little slack, and then a bold, unbelieving gangster could manage to assemble an army and usurp power, of course again by violent means. Religion, ever opportunistic, protecting its own turf, usually did not hesitate to transfer its allegiance to the new ruler and proclaim *him* God-appointed. Gangsterism solemnly sanctified.

In a modified way this is still the case in our time, and definitely in the recent past. Think of European kings and emperors being crowned by bishops, with the nod of the Pope. Think of presidents and prime ministers invoking divine help any chance they get, and certainly if they think people are watching. Think of religious functionaries blessing weapons. A bishop spraying holy water on an instrument of destruction such as a tank, invoking God's blessings, is very likely the most obscene tableau the World will ever see. The close connection between Government and Religion was never really completely severed.

Religion, with its fables of heaven and hell, plays a major role in our thinking. Its dogmas supply docile, ignorant participants, afraid of a Deity who watches their every step, judging their behavior accordingly. Heaven, according to the Book, is a reward for being good (read: no threat to Government) and Hell a punishment for being bad (read: suspicious or envious of the ruling class and therefore rebellious). Participating in a war is seen as honorable, looked upon with favor by the Deity. Think of the rewards for bravery, equated with purity of heart. The ultimate sacrifice, death, is made into the greatest achievement a brave soldier can attain. Again, Religion is the big influence here. The top echelon, doing their appointed thing, makes sure that dying on the battlefield has an aura of holiness; there is no doubt that the fallen have earned their place in heaven and are welcomed by the Deity himself. A cross on the soldier's grave attests to it.

As a rule, the leaders of Religion were happy to limit their involvement in politics to supporting and glorifying the king, making him God-like, whoever he may have been at the time. Their support was rewarded with the usual perks: tax-free status and social glorification. Lately, however, signs are appearing indicating a desire by some religious functionaries to again be directly involved in ruling the world, even employing violence, if need be.

A strong, exclusive bond existed in earlier times between the King and his religious and military departments. Sometimes it was one person comprising all three roles: King/Priest/Commander-in-Chief.

The Military Industrial Religious complex, MIRC, under its generic name "Government," must be seen as a giant octopus, which has the World (us) firmly in the grip of its tentacles. With a smile, its mouth spews forth lie after lie, each one based on the previous one and thereby strengthened. The biggest one, of course, is the one of going to heaven after death. Without this enormous lie, MIRC would have a hard time getting impressionable youngsters to die "for their country" or to commit suicide "for their faith."

Moses and the God

Although it is not certain that in history there ever was the *Biblical* man called Moses, for purposes of this book about the Book we will consider that there was.

The Book explains that a God exists and that he has a name, YHWH. The name appears for the first time in Exodus 6:3, when The God confronts and "says" to him that in the past he used to appear to Abraham, Isaac and Jacob, who knew him only as God Almighty, but not by his proper name. Moses used the language of the Hebrews; consequently the name of The God became a Hebrew expression.

Moses claimed that God spoke to him, urging him to persuade the Pharaoh to let the oppressed people called Israel leave Egypt. Moses seemed reluctant at first, but even when the Pharaoh refused permission he kept trying. He also needed to convince the Elders of the various Hebrew tribes that The God had spoken to him on a one-to-one basis. Did he decide on the name YHWH, because of the connection with Abraham, etc., and was he therefore able to convince the Elders that he was referring to the same Deity, because the name means "I am who I was and will be"?

A mystery

There is a mystery attached to this narration in the Book of Exodus: Moses goes to great lengths to give a Name to The God, but he does not at any time give us the name of the Pharaoh, giving rise to speculation as to who this Ruler was. But if such important information is not forthcoming, it raises doubt as to the veracity of the story. Possibly Ezra and Nehemiah found it safer not to identify the Pharaoh, since it could be researched later on.

In the Book's narrative, Moses was adopted by a daughter of the unnamed Pharaoh, so this ruler was in effect his stepgrandfather. Apparently, he walked in and out of the palace at will. We can also assume that the Pharaoh knew that Moses was not just any Hebrew, but one who had escaped the edict of killing all male Hebrew children at the time of their birth. Why would he even be tolerated in the Pharaoh's presence?

That brings up a valid question: Did a character like Moses ever exist?

If he did exist, we can assume that as a citizen of Egypt he had access to the great libraries of the known world. It appears that Moses spoke the language of Egypt as well as Hebrew and had extensive knowledge of written and oral history. It is also clear that Moses could read and write, which gave him an enormous advantage, as not many of the people were literate.

As mentioned earlier, there is no archaeological evidence that an event such as the Exodus occurred in Egypt, neither is there is a record of it in what we would call the history books of that country. However, even if it *did* occur it is unlikely that a story of this kind would be reported in Egypt's annals—kings rather boast of sieges than admit defeats.

The account, or the myth, definitely became part of the folklore of the nation of Israel which much later came into written expression in the Book's narration. There is no doubt that the story was meant to stress monotheism and strengthen the ties with the Supreme Being in the people's minds. But the thought arises that the authors might have made it all up, even the existence of an ancient nation of Israel itself. Archaeology does not at this time support that such a nation existed in the time it was reported.

However, there is another possibility that is worthy of consideration. The Book often concerns itself with long-range predictions, sometimes spanning millennia. Its main subject matter is the prediction of a total change in the world's political setup.

There are other ways of looking at the Pharaoh mystery. Different Pharaohs may have been involved. The one who ordered the killing of Jewish babies may not have been the same as the one Moses dealt with later on. "Pharaoh," in the context, may be no more than a term indicating political power. But, even if this were so, it seems strange that one particular Pharaoh would not be aware of the decrees and doings of another, and that the writers of the story did not take that into consideration.

Therefore, the story of the exodus from Egypt may be one of the symbols for relief from oppression, referring to the bondage existing in today's world's system and the promise of a way out: the relief brought about by The God and his perfect government. The Book is replete with references to that effect. If this is the reality, we can conclude that the Book is definitely not an historical record, but a compendium of stories designed to alert us to the fact that we are indeed oppressed, perhaps without realizing it, by an unnatural System based on illegitimate power, greed and superstition.

Pitfalls of power

We can read about abuse of power in the book of Samuel (1Samuel 10-18). During the prophet Samuel's tenure as a judge, the people of Israel wanted a king to be appointed, in order to be like other nations they admired. No other nation existed with an invisible king and they felt left out, ashamed, afraid of ridicule. The world, they thought, was watching, and the world's opinion was what counted. Samuel warned them about what such a ruler would demand of them. It is interesting reading. It gives a good picture of what power will do to an individual elevated to such a position.

Samuel knew the pitfalls of power firsthand. It seems that the people had hoped that one of Samuel's sons would be qualified to lead, like their father, whose impartiality was greatly respected. But when Samuel had appointed his sons, Joel and Abia, as judges in Beersheba, they proved to be no better than crooked politicians. They took bribes and circumvented the Law.

In spite of all the wisdom and experience he shared with the populace, Samuel's warnings went unheeded; he was eventually forced to appoint a king anyway. That's how Israel became one of the nations with its own human ruler, bypassing an unhappy Yahweh, who felt rejected. Yahweh, according to Samuel, had said: They did not reject *you*, they rejected *me*. But when trouble starts they don't have to come back to me about it. I am not going to listen to complaints." It proved to be prophetic; trouble came quickly.

The conclusion is that the stories in the Book, although not historically correct, are socially correct. We don't need to reconcile the Book with history, because there is not really a connection. The Book exists by itself. It is, in essence, Yahweh's Book. The impact it may have on the individual is private, and such a person's consequential actions do not validate the information one way or the other.

Stories and phantasms

The Book tells stories. The stories are not necessarily reports of actual happenings. They can only be seen as symbols of situations occurring in our world, sometimes announced many thousands of years ahead of time. There is no way to prove that the stories of Abraham, Isaac, Jacob, Moses and the exodus from Egypt rest on historical evidence.

An example of the need to escape from a bad situation was told in the Book's story of the Hebrew people: Through a dramatic series of events, the clan of Heber, or the Hebrews, had become trapped in the country of Egypt, where they were treated as virtual slaves by the Pharaoh, or king, of the period in which this supposedly took place.

Pharaohs are used in the Book to depict the World's governments, ruled by people who think of themselves either as chosen by God or being gods themselves. The Pharaoh was presented to the people as the god *Horus* in human form, and because of his supposed link to a Deity, he had absolute power over his subjects. The enslaved Hebrews were a cheap source of labor and the present Pharaoh, who is not identified in the story, did not permit them to leave.

It is probable that the Pharaohs descended from one of Adam's children, or that their rise to power was the result of a takeover. We do know that the Egyptian rulers followed the course taken by Adam and Eve and acted in opposition to Yahweh, who had said that sinners would positively die. They had taken the Babylonian phantasm of going-to-heaven-and-meeting-God to a great height.

Their bodies were mummified to protect them from decay, probably to defy the pronouncement: "Dust you are, and to dust you will return." The mummification process requires removal of the organs, to assist preservation of the rest of the body. The brain was removed by tearing it out through the nose. It was the ultimate insult, since the brain is the seat of the spirit that makes a person a person. The body was then filled with resin to keep its shape and wrapped in strips of linen. It was thought that the body had to be preserved for the soul to go to heaven. Phantasm upon phantasm.

The Chosen

The Hebrew people had descended from Abraham, who allegedly had a covenant with Yahweh, who had promised to protect him and make him the father of a great nation. He had also given him the land of Canaan (Genesis 12: 1-7). The clan of the Hebrews became trapped in Egypt, were treated as slaves, and they saw no way out of their predicament. Then Moses appeared.

Moses was working as a shepherd who one day was met by Yahweh on the mountain of Horeb. The God commanded him to confront the present Pharaoh and tell him to let the Hebrews go. When Moses expressed doubt that he, a simple shepherd, could demand such a thing, Yahweh assured him he would assist him and be successful. Moses did as he was told. When the Pharaoh refused at first, the country was struck with one plague after another, until he finally acceded to set the Hebrews free.

The story is told to impress upon the reader or listener that Yahweh, The God, is more powerful than any of the world's political forces. It appears that the Hebrews were "chosen" by Yahweh to show that he could indeed free people from oppression. "Chosen," however, did not mean that they were considered to be better than others, or that The God favored them above others. More likely it meant that they had the same traits that the majority of people have and therefore could be used as an example people, a prototype.

The fact that they needed help to be rescued from the land of Egypt made them the perfect choice. However, as time progressed they proved they could be as stubborn, arrogant, ungrateful, mean, unfaithful and headstrong as any of us. It is also clear that they lost the protection of Yahweh long ago, when they became part of the World's political system. The Israelis may claim to still be his chosen or favorite people, but there is no way that they will ever again enjoy the kind of protection they received when they supposedly left Egypt. They are now just one of the Nations.

However, historically sound or not, the story was meant to show that The God is capable of overcoming the World's ideologies, and that he intends to do just that.

The Book is an advertisement about Yahweh, by and for Yahweh, touting his extraordinary power and his willingness to give protection to those who choose to be his "Israelites, his "people."

Noah

The Book's story of Noah has no basis in fact either, as far as scholars, scientists and archaeologists have determined; it is a combination of numerous other flood myths from a variety of cultures, practically all derived from Babylonian and Sumerian sources. Ziusudra, Atrahasis and Utnapishtim were similar characters escaping from a watery calamity. It would be interesting to know which was the original and which was a copy, or a copy of a copy.

A tablet was found dating from about 1200 B.C., describing the Gilgamesh experience, with Utnapishtim in the role of Noah. Hebrew priests would argue, of course, that this narration was based upon the Noah account which was handed down orally through the ages, copied by the pagans in Babylon, omitting Yahweh, and ascribing major and minor roles to members of their multi-member god list. Enu, Ea, Enlil, Ishtar, Ashur, Shamash, Shulmanu, Tammuz, Hadad, Sin, Dagan, Ninurta, Nisroch, Nergal, Tiamat, Bel and Marduk were among the 2,100 deities mentioned in the story.

The water cycle was represented by a rain god, a thunder god, a lightning god and a wind god. Now that we know that no such gods are involved in nature's workings, monotheism seems like a more ingenious proposition. Some writers added their own ending. Utnapishtim gained immortality and was transported "far away." No one has seen or heard from him since. You might with some justification think that obtaining immortality would be an occurrence important enough to not lose track of such a person and show his face on CNN now and then. Nothing is too far away for a camera crew these days.

In the story of Noah, so says the Book, the Flood destroyed all of mankind; and through Noah's sons Shem, Ham and Japheth, the whole world was repopulated. Neither ending seems plausible if we take this as historical reporting. However, if we see it as a far-ranging prediction, as often is the case in the Book, pertaining to the times of the end, it becomes much clearer. If the new "Israel" is a nation of individuals gathered together from all races and nationalities, the reference to Shem, Ham and Japheth makes a lot more sense.

Arabs, Blacks, Asians and Caucasians from all nations of the world, forming a special, "peculiar" (holy) remnant of mankind, will start anew and from them the whole earth will be repopulated with living souls.

Since we are not concerned here with comparing the Book's stories with archaeological or scientific findings, or what is fact and what is not, and are only reporting what the Book says, consider what could have been transpiring if the story of Noah were true.

First of all, it is well to realize that all activity on earth is executed by humans. Gods are seldom directly involved. Humans are guided by certain principles, which make the outcome of their machinations either good or bad. What inspired Noah to do what he did? Who or what told him that a calamity of huge proportions would take place? Afterwards, why was he reassured when he saw the *rainbow*?

The answers to these questions depend on whether or not we realize that nature at that time must have been radically different from what we now perceive it to be. We see a blue sky, now and then partially or wholly covered with clouds, and we assume that it has always been this way. It rains on occasion, some places more than others; we see an occasional rainbow and we do not give the matter a second thought. However, when we scrutinize the Book more closely, we have to come to the conclusion it was not always so.

Why did Noah build a huge vessel? It certainly was no river raft, given its size. There was no body of water large enough in his area to launch the enormous ship into.

Now this: It seems likely that it had never rained on that part of the planet, even though there was a thick, permanent cloud cover, and that vegetation received its water through a *vapor that went up from the earth,* as the Book informs us. Why then did Noah decide to build an ark? What did he know to tell him that a catastrophic flood would occur and how did he come by this knowledge? The Book says that God "told him." Since it is unlikely that he spoke directly to God or God directly to him, something else must have been going on.

All activity taking place on the planet is influenced by an idea, an urge, an ideology, an understanding, a quest for knowledge, a wish to satisfy a need, or a condition, etc.

"God spoke to Noah" meant that Noah, like a prophet for Yahweh, thinking about things that went on around him, saw a calamity in the making. A flood is the result of too much water, and there may have been a quest for knowledge about the way water vapor came to be produced day after day, year after year.

Certain scientists in the days of Noah may have been experimenting with probes into the cloud cover to find out how the system worked. Noah may even have been one of them. Scientists can double as prophets, as can anyone else.

As an added bonus they may have wished to visit their dead relatives in heaven, above the clouds, as they had been led to believe by their religious managers.

Noah could have realized that a dangerous experiment was in the works and used his reasoning powers to calculate how much water would be involved if the experiment succeeded.

He may have understood that Yahweh was unhappy with the behavior of the *specials* (the progeny of Adam) he had created and that he had decided to teach them a lesson. The *flood* that followed was not worldwide, but limited to the general area of Mesopotamia. It wiped out all the *specials*, except Noah and his family.

The rainbow significance

When the calamity had ended, and Noah saw a rainbow in the sky, he understood that the Flood could never be repeated. The permanent cloud cover, instrumental in the deluge, had always obscured the sun. It was now gone and Noah saw direct sunlight for the first time in his life, the rainbow phenomenon not being possible without sunlight and a rain shower.

The diet adjustment

Another remarkable item in the Book is the announcement of a drastic change in people's diet after the Flood. In Genesis 9:3 we learn that it was now all right to eat the flesh of animals. Until that day only vegetation is mentioned as food for man and beast. Did direct sunlight change the composition of vegetation? It may have been closer to animal protein before, which made a diet adjustment necessary.

Noah's legacy

Today the circumstances also indicate that things are far from normal and that a catastrophe may be imminent. "It will be as in the days of Noah," the Book predicts (Luke 17:26, Matthew 24:37), pointing not to another Flood, but at the comparison with a central issue in Noah's days: "the earth was filled with *violence"* (Gen 6:13). Today's escalating wars, the fight between religious convictions, the climate change, the economic situation, the hunger, the incurable diseases, all point to a coming climax.

Much effort has been directed towards finding Noah's Ark, with no provable result. There are *claims* of a result. Part of a "structure" found on Mount Ararat is supposed to be the remnants of the Ark; for political reasons (military, no doubt) no one is allowed to further investigate. The conclusion may be drawn that the mighty ship never was, its existence to be compared with the Garden of Eden, that the two stories are only a means of pointing out the facts of life to us, a reminder to seek shelter before it is too late.

The nature of Religion

What scientists and archaeologists perceive as ancient or prehistoric "religion" may not necessarily be the phenomenon we know today, because the exact belief systems prevalent in the earlier years are not known. "Temples" may not originally have been houses of worship. It is more believable that they were structures to ward off evil spirits, or evil beasts such as wild boars and scorpions. Natural forces were feared, and it is extremely unlikely that monotheism was part of the organized belief setup. The organized system of religion that we know today may have evolved slowly. However, it was firmly established around 1867 B.C., in the heyday of *Babylon*, the city-state on the banks of the Euphrates River, which region, in the Bible, is used as the personification of idolatry. Most of the "great" religions of the world owe their beliefs to the inventions and myths of Babylonian rulers.

Babylonian religion is a purposeful hoax. It wants us to believe things that have no basis in truth or fact. It grew from attempts by primitive, superstitious people to explain life and death. Myths had forever been a staple in the beliefs of the indigenous population, as a response to fear about things they had no control over.

All the forces of nature were unpredictable and death was a terrifying mystery. Each force of nature had its own god or goddess. Rain, wind, thunder, trees, rocks—all could have their own particular god. To exploit this superstition, images of the various gods and goddesses—made of wood, stone or other material—were placed in temples and presented to the gullible people as their deities. To accommodate the various beliefs the indigenous population entertained about their gods it was considered acceptable that the gods resided simultaneously in buildings and in the natural forces they embodied. It was known, even six thousand years ago, that people will believe anything and certainly if it is dressed up as religion.

Temples were the homes of the gods and were run by priests collecting offerings, sacrifices and anything else to keep the god alive and happy. The gods were given increased importance by the priests as time went by. This was enthusiastically encouraged by Government.

The authorities made people believe that priests had contact with the various Gods, and urged them to donate food and services to please and serve the particular Deity. Doing this gave the population the feeling that they could at least do *something* about their plight. At one time in Babylon there were as over two thousand deities to choose from. The food donations and other services rendered to the gods also meant a steady source of income and a continuous pool of manpower for the rulers. Temples were often combined with granaries, all owned and run by the authorities.

Today, anyone can start a religion. This is called, at least in the Western world, *Freedom of Religion*. Governments encourage the creation of new religious factions. They love different types of religion, the more varieties the better. Profusion is synonymous with confusion, and confusion is the name of the game. Confusion means control. Anyone who has an idea about something that has the potential to be called a "Faith," can become a preacher, using any pretext, and from that moment on is considered a holy man. Religious denominations are gratefully rewarded with a tax-exempt status and an exalted position in the community. Who would dare to tax God?

However, Freedom of Religion also means that there is ample opportunity for weirdness. Religion itself may be hijacked again by some who preach violence to get their religious or political view across. Freedom of religion dictates that such a fanatical ideology must then be tolerated by those who have peaceful co-existence in mind. Because of the enormous psychological influence exerted by religious officers, members of an otherwise peaceful community may easily be led into believing that their leaders know better, and join in the fracas.

Fabricated Religion causes most of the unrest in the world and this will, paradoxically, be the reason for its own undoing. When Religion loses its credibility and fails, as predicted in the Book of Revelation, it will bring down the world's way of doing things, its governments, its finances, its core beliefs. The glue, the Big Lie (snake talk!) that held the status quo together will be gone, and their world will collapse. It will also convince those who had turned their backs on the flawed system that they were right in rejecting its insidious influence.

The Big Lie, BIGGEST fruit of all

Lies, by definition, are efforts to obscure the truth. It is well known that any lie, if repeated often enough, will eventually become accepted truth. Religious lies are served to us with a pious front, often by people clothed in elaborate dress and hats, designed to impress the superstitious and make the lies more believable. The life-after-death scenario, with its literal heaven with God on a throne, waiting for us with open arms, is not supported by any statements in the Book, although many, without checking, believe that it is.

Going to heaven is perceived by the public at large as a very desirable opportunity. Promoting this idea was the shrewdest move the Government/Religion Combo ever made. The concept caught on wholesale in the days of Babylon and is still believed to be God's own truth. It is the mother of all lies. The promise of life after death for everyone, in heaven, makes Organized Religion a true cult of death, because heaven-as-a-place does not exist. It is no coincidence that Death in the Western world is symbolized by a cross, itself the symbol Organized Religion uses to identify itself and its personnel in the Western world.

"Heaven" is not a large building with enormous rooms, where God resides surrounded by his angels, along with all the deceased that have accumulated over the years. It is not a geographical place but a metaphor for a state of excellence, perfection, loftiness, and high principles. God is everywhere, and the word "high" does not indicate a distance from the surface of our planet to a location somewhere above the clouds. Therefore, it follows that we—or some ethereal part of us—do not *go* to heaven after we die. There is nothing in any of the writings to indicate such a pleasant outcome or that we will automatically go into a state of perfection when dead. The Book makes it very clear that dead is dead—at least for now—no matter what your religious manager says. No pearly gates for anyone.

In so-called Christianity the idea exists that heaven is a realm, a place where God lives with his angels and where he receives the souls of those whose earthly life has come to an end.

Jesus, who knew that the religious leaders of his day believed and fostered this idea, taunted them with his parable of the rich man and Lazarus, who respectively ended up in Hades and Heaven. The rich man saw that Lazarus was being attended to by Abraham and asked for some relief for his parched lips—of course caused by the hellfire. The irony and the sarcasm embedded in the parable escaped the Sadducees, and the story became proof of the existence of a literal heaven and a hell. However, nowhere else in the Book is there even the slightest hint that this situation touches reality. It would override the proclamation of the resurrection. The two concepts are too far apart to be able to exist side by side.

The world's definition of "soul" is not supported by the Book. Souls are living, breathing units and include man, beast, birds, fish, etc. The idea that we *have* a soul, separate from our body, and that the souls of *good* people will go to a Heaven, where God awaits them with open arms as if they were long-lost children, is a total tongue-in-cheek fabrication by illegitimate Government. So is the idea of Hell, where the souls of *bad* people are deposited, to be tortured forever and ever. It is all snake talk.

There are two ways of looking at this phenomenon. If the snake talk is seen as coming from Satan as an individual person, with his own agenda, then one should give credit where credit is due. Because to fabricate the scenario that a "soul"(basically "a breathing being") will go to heaven at the moment of death and have such a lie be believed by billions of people is no small feat. It shows Satan's cleverness, his deviousness, and how much insight he has into the human psyche.

Firstly, he knew that for a lie to be believed it had better be a whopper.

Secondly, playing upon our vanity, our arrogance and our spiritual laziness he succeeded in leading us around the garden path for thousands of years, knowing we'd rather not think of the alternative, death without parole.

But if we see him as representing our own arrogant inclinations, combined with wishful thinking, we will come to the understanding how much we are deceiving ourselves and that blaming Satan is really picking a scapegoat.

What the Book actually says is that nothing will happen when we die, at least not right away (Eccl. 9:5-10). It speaks of going to sleep in death, hidden in the "grave" (sometimes transliterated "hell") until Resurrection Day, when everyone, good or bad, will be made to live again, and judged. It also says that those who don't make the grade will then be eliminated, destroyed, never to appear again to make life on earth miserable for the living souls.

At that time, the Book informs the reader, a new, legitimate Government will be established *on earth:* a Government "*of* Heaven," not to be confused with "*in* Heaven." The Book calls it the Heavenly Kingdom of the true God. Heaven, or heavenly indicates that it will be perfect, and has nothing whatever to do with a place somewhere in space.

That this will be *on earth* is the very last thing Government wants you to become aware of. It means that they will be out of power, and maybe judged unfavorably. That's where Religion was brought in: to confuse this message by every means possible.

All Religions touting a life-after-death-in-heaven scenario take their cue from Babylon. They may just be parroting the globally accepted beliefs, but that does not make them less guilty. There is nothing to stop them from using their own eyes and brain to look up the information in the Book, which also mentions a *Spirit* behind all this.

Knowing the World as we all do, and going along with the familiar way it has been run for thousands of years, it is difficult to accept that we have been lulled into a kind of religious stupor, to accept the idea that nothing will ever change. What you see today, you will see tomorrow. The reality, however, is different. We have very effectively been brainwashed in order to give our leaders the chance to strive for more control, more wealth, more power. We are blinded from noticing that our religious leaders are actually hand-in-glove with our political leaders to achieve mutual goals. We fail to see this, because our attention is constantly diverted from the essentials by the lies we receive from the authorities, sometimes even in the daily news broadcasts.

The Book explains the essentials as follows: As inhabitants of our planet earth, we could have had a good life, right here, were it not for our wise leaders; a life without pain, strife, uncertainty and confusion; free from wars, diseases, money worries—and, in the end, free from the death curse itself.

Life after death, and angels

The Book tells us about life after death and leaves no doubt that it is not going to be in heaven, or anywhere else but on earth.

Mankind is part of the creation, of which the earth was a result. Why would people end up somewhere else than on planet earth, which was made for them? The fact that we only live to be a hundred may give us the idea that we are here only temporarily, for a very short period, after which a different situation takes over, but that is pure fantasy. The planet with its flora and fauna is an ideal abode for creatures like us, and there is no necessity for an alternative.

Luke 20:34 gives some indication of what life on earth would be like. Jesus was answering trick questions about the resurrection, put to him by Sadducees, religious leaders who did not believe in it. Resurrection presents an impossible hurdle for Religion, which has an opposing agenda not based on reality. Their agenda must be seen as a police action, undertaken in the service of Government, which brought Religion to life for this purpose.

Jesus said that those who survived the resurrection will be like angels in heaven. What he did *not* say was that they would become angels living in heaven. They would be *like* angels in heaven, in that they would no longer die. Heaven is a metaphor for greatness, perfection. Perfect beings receive eternal life—"perfect" meaning "in tune with the future," rejecting the present World, convinced of the possibility of a better one.

Do not get the impression from the above that angels *cannot* die. They, like all things invisible, are synonymous with thoughts. Lucifer (Satan) was an Angel of Light until he became an Angel of Darkness. If he is the expression of our own arrogant thoughts and self-important inclinations, it follows that angels are thoughts, influences on our behavior: products of the mind. It also means that, once we change our mind about things, certain "bad angels" no longer occupy a place in our thought processes and are then in effect "dead." These particular thoughts no longer stand in the way of acquiring, and hanging on to, eternal life.

Every dead angel brings us a step closer to being accepted as citizens of the new world with its new heavens (the new style of government).

Another interesting item is that men will no longer marry and women no longer be given in marriage. That, taken together with the mention of incorruptible bodies in 1 Cor. 15:53, suggests that our sex life will no longer be the same. Once the correct number of citizens of Yahweh's "people" has been reached, reproduction is no longer necessary. In the promised perfect world, overpopulation is not on the menu. A considerable, but limited amount of citizens can live on the planet, providing abundance without causing damage to the environment. Yahweh is not a God of poverty.

One can only come to the conclusion that sex will not be eliminated altogether, but that it will be changed, and an improvement over what we have now. With our limited understanding it is difficult to imagine how it could be enriched. Sex taken to a higher level can only mean that, when differences between the sexes no longer exist, the physical act will be replaced by a more intellect-oriented one, and therefore also produce a different result. It is practically blasphemy to suggest that sex, or whatever it is then called, will ever be less awesome and interesting—let's not underestimate The God.

How and why did prophets come to be convinced that resurrection was a reality? They probably considered all the proffered possibilities and found them all wanting. In one way or another they did not see justice and fairness there—hallmarks of Yahweh. After all, he is, as Moses had explained, a God of the living, not of the dead. How to deal with all those who had passed away and never had a chance to hear about Yahweh because of the official concealment of the Name? The times of the end had been very well documented. The conclusion was that a period *had to* occur when everybody who ever lived was present and confronted with the choice: stay with the established norm or turn it down. That could only mean one thing: in order to make an intelligent choice those must be made to live again in a time where a system of communication with sight and sound was part of daily life, allowing them to see the results of six thousand years of mismanagement.

In 1804 the earth's population stood at 1 billion. It was doubled in 1927 (123 years), and doubled again around 1970 (43 years). On October 31, 2011 (41 years), it had risen to seven billion, with a daily increase of 209,000.

It has been calculated that there are now more people living on earth than all those combined in the past 6000 years. Television and other electronic media give nobody an opportunity to escape observing what the world is about.

Is the present overpopulation actually the resurrection—a method to separate the sheep from the goats? Resurrection and Judgment may be going on right now, under our very noses.

Good and bad people

So, what is the difference between good and bad people, according to Government and Organized Religion?

A good person agrees with Government and swallows everything Religion dishes up. Rocking the boat of the system is frowned upon.

A bad person questions authority and uses his brain to decide if what his government and religious managers tell him could possibly be true.

It was to Government's and Religion's mutual advantage to confuse and misinform their constituents, keeping them timid, obedient to those in power, afraid to do "wrong." And although not everyone believes the official explanation, there is no argument that the uncertainty and confusion about what happens after we die wields terrible power over the majority of people.

Religion's fable of Heaven as a reward for being *good* promises peace of mind and tranquility, but it harasses and extorts instead.

The Book has a different view. It separates the righteous and the unrighteous and calls the unrighteous "the wicked," who will be destroyed come resurrection time.

Immortal soul

The word-combination "immortal soul" does not appear anywhere in the Book. It certainly is a reflection of Adam and Eve's superiority complex, thinking that they would become like gods. The gateway to heaven was their imagined way out of their realizing that they were now dead people walking. We can only guess whether they believed it themselves; the idea may have developed over the years. However, we can be assured that the Lie will be embraced by Government and Religion as long as possible. This is logical, because they know that without it their system would collapse. For the time being they can rest easy. The fabrication is so strongly embedded in people's conscience that it will be most difficult to convince the masses that it is a lie, pure and simple.

One can only marvel at the brilliance of the concept and how it created indescribable power over the majority of people. Consider what it accomplished:

- A docile population, afraid of being "bad"
- Protection for the king/priest, whose reign was perceived as "from God"

- A strong, permanent bond between grateful rulers and the religious institutions
- An unending supply of soldiers, because fighting for the king was perceived to be similar to fighting for God
- Yahweh out of the picture, seen as a hindrance for the "progress" of the world

The strength of the invention kept the truth concealed for thousands of years and is ongoing. It shows Satan at his best. It made "him" the true god of this world. The going-to-heaven scenario enables governments to raise armies of young, impressionable boys to fight for various "ideals." Any ideal will do, but the ones that work best are defense of freedom, defense of worship, love of god and country, defending the status quo, the way of life. The implication is that God favors those who sacrifice their lives for their king and country, and certainly for their religious beliefs.

False Religion is intrinsically wicked and opportunistic. It will support any established government whether benign or evil. Don't forget that in Babylonian times the king ("lugal")—was also the chief priest; he claimed to be related to God, or to be God himself, and that that was the reason for his terrible hold on the people. He could recruit any available man if he wanted to have something built, or to establish an army to go on raids to conquer other communities and increase his hold over more territory and resources. More wealth also meant more stockpiles of the latest weaponry.

Government and religion, hand in hand, caused the establishment of walled cities, city states and later countries, or what the bible scornfully calls "the nations."

Quite possibly the foregoing is all myth. Certainly the creation story has been picked apart by scientists and sundry other learned people. Maybe Adam and Eve never existed as persons and were only symbols for certain situations. However, the chronology used in the Book makes it very likely that the very real happenings in the Ubaid period, supported by archaeology, are consistent with "eating the forbidden fruit": the start of large-scale agriculture, the establishment of walled cities and centralized governments, the often warlike situation between the various city states and the attempts to unify the area under one rule, pointing to the desire to create a World Government. Hammurabi was one of the earliest rulers who more or less succeeded in this effort, but it did not last.

It could of course be a coincidence, but it would be a most remarkable one.

Sin, one of the early fruits of Eden

In most comic strips, someone desires to dominate the World: the bad guy. He is usually defeated in his quest for world dominance by a good guy. Superman, Batman and Spiderman are some of the good guys that come to mind. The good people always win; the bad guys never. A comic strip deals with fantasy, not reality. In the world of reality the ultimate bad guy, Satan, has won, and won big. Sin is the name of the game in the World.

What constitutes sin? What do we really know about this "person," Satan, the Devil, who apparently urges us to sin? We have been introduced to him in the Book, wherein he has been given a bad name, because he does bad things and is said to be making others do bad things as well. He has been called the Opposer, the Deceiver, the *Misleader,* the Dragon, the Serpent, and Beelzebub, sometimes depicted as a form of God. Apparently, he is a fallen angel who at one time was an "Angel of Light," with the name of "Lucifer." We also learn that, when he "quarreled" with God, he was "thrown out of Heaven," together with a number of equally bad angels, and hurled "down." What was the nature of their quarrel?

Heaven, believed to be "up," is the place where God lives with his angels. People who lead "good" lives will go there, as any religious person will tell you, and will live there forever.

On the other hand, the Devil, with his set of erring angels, lives in "Hell," believed to be "down," a fiery place where he torments those who have been leading "bad" lives, *forever*. The strange part about this is that those he torments can only be designated as his obedient *followers*, because they have been leading bad lives at his urging. What's going on here? Why is it so important to him to fill his Hell with bad people? Is this part of the World's reality comic strip?

Lately, the belief in a literal Hell seems to have abated somewhat, probably because we are not as naive as those who lived five hundred years ago, who could neither read nor write and depended on what their religious leaders told them to believe. More and better communications have changed the perception of a great many. But with the new ideas about hell came new questions. What to believe *instead?* Is the Devil still around? Is he still making us commit sins? What, really, are the bad things called "Sin"?

The Devil may be a person, but he could also very well be a *personification*—the personification of our combined vanity, misplaced pride, arrogance, lust for power, and ignorance. The writers of the Bible, after much trying, may have discovered he could easier be identified were these traits distilled down and combined into a single angelic being—angelic in the sense of invisibility, not high quality of character.

The people on this earth are ill-equipped to deal with an ultra-smart angel like Satan. "He" preys on our longing for center-of-the-universe importance, coupled with our desire to be like gods, to rule the World the way we think it should be ruled, thereby luring us away from things that really matter. Clever as we think we are, however, we do not easily realize that we are being manipulated by a force much cleverer than we can ever hope to be.

That is why the whole area of "good" and "bad" and "sin"

and "evil" needs to be analyzed. Because "bad" and "good" has a lot to do with the way we worship and how we experience our Deity. What is the nature of our "badness"? Are we "bad" individually or are we "bad" as a group?

The word "bad" is not synonymous with "evil" or "wicked."

Bad has the meaning of "wrong," while evil is *intentionally doing wrong*. It shows a state of mind bent on performing evil deeds, while "bad" points more in the direction of a wrong decision made in good faith maybe caused by ignorance for innocent reasons.

The wicked

The Book has a lot to say about "the wicked," and how they will be dealt with in the times of the end.

What constitutes wickedness? Who are the wicked? They can hardly be what we think of as people with bad behavior, like stealing, murdering, raping or worse. We don't need the Book to tell us that; everybody knows that such people are bad news. But percentagewise there are very few of us who are guilty of crimes of such magnitude. It must be obvious to anyone that this relatively small group of evildoers is not the one pinpointed in the Book, although they probably won't qualify for life in the new world.

"Wicked" must have a specific meaning for Yahweh. He resents being shoved aside, and considers anyone doing that as wicked, or godless. One could regard "wicked" as a religious concept only.

Serving false gods, having disregard for his laws of nature, laughing at the pronouncements of his prophets, unwilling to take instruction, condoning the behavior of the nations with their propensity for violence, having faith in the world's political and religious rulers, may well be the wickedness he is referring to (Psalm 146:3-4).

Living on the planet means that we are practically in daily

contact with the world's ways, its practices, its belief systems and its politics. It seems impossible to avoid involvement one way or another. Having a government seems to be a necessary evil; ignoring it completely is out of the question.

But we can disassociate ourselves from actively participating, or even entertaining the idea that the world's rulers are God's legitimate agents who should be held in reverence because they are in the position they are in. It is true that they would not be there if Yahweh did not allow them to occupy their particular "throne" for a while, but admiring them because of their prowess is probably not looked at with his approval.

Does that mean that, apart from being "sinners" we could also be classified as "wicked," because our options are limited? Probably not. Given Yahweh's sense of reasonableness, I would think that we have a good chance of being exonerated from adverse judgment *because* of these limited options. Could we have prevented Alexander the Great from starting the largest political empire in the ancient world? Or have stopped "Saint" Constantine from waging war because he saw a cross in the sky by which he would conquer?

If there is indeed a Day of Judgment, our limitations will protect us from destruction. It may be enough to recognize the threat and then try to keep our involvement to a minimum (Romans 12:2).

The Book may imply that someone deliberately choosing to disregard Yahweh's commandments and laws is "evil," but that is only a religious concept.

As to the Great Lie, the serpent (Satan) in Genesis 3:4 says to the woman: "You positively will not die." One could argue that that was an evil, wicked statement, because Satan knew better, making the Lie a deliberate fraud, with far-reaching implications to this day. The serpent was deliberately evil, his listener and follower was only his victim, although she could not claim ignorance. But it does show the need for discernment—to know who we are dealing with.

When the Lie became universally accepted dogma, one could further argue that someone believing the Lie is equally evil. However, in the absence of better information for a majority of the people, because of Government and Religious propaganda against scrutiny, such a believer is not evil, but could be labeled "bad," because believing without an intellectual basis is a meaningless exercise. "Wrong" can be excused, "evil" cannot. Being bad is not a question of morality, as Religion and Government would like you to believe, but of discernment.

One can be a moral person without the involvement of some religion. But look at the many evil deeds performed in the name of Religion itself, insinuating that God is involved. That's why I argue that Religion is intrinsically evil, opportunistic, and devoid of morality, making it the perfect companion for Government's lust for people manipulation. This can be brought to the fore in many different ways, making it seem repetitive. But because Government and Religion have influenced so many aspects of our existence it may need a reminder now and then.

The Book, in many places, tells us about "the end of the world," and that God is angry with us, because we are sinners. It is generally believed that the end will come about in a violent way, perhaps as the result of a nuclear war, as we strive to blow our planet to bits. (With the best of intentions, of course). Is *this* information to be trusted?

The Book says that Satan is the one who misleads the whole inhabited earth (Rev. 12:9). He tempts us to sin. So, we must define what sin really is. Is it possible that we are being misled on a huge scale? All of us together? In concert?

The World consists of many nations, each one with its own set of laws and sometimes with its own brand of religion. We have been given the impression that is the way the Creator had planned it, and how he wants it. The World's propaganda machine says so. It may be wrong. Agreeing with the way the World is put together, or "belonging" to it, going along with its violent ways, trusting the world's religious leaders who support it, sanction it, and profit by it, may well be the sinning the Book refers to.

If this sounds strange, consider what the World has been made us believe:

- There is only one God (1 Cor 8:5, King James).
- He is all Love, ever-forgiving, never angry enough to kill anyone.
- He is in charge at the United Nations, guiding the world as best he can.
- When we die, we'll go to heaven and stay with God, our Creator, forever (Eccl 9:5-10, KJ).
- When we pray for anything at all, God listens and does something about it.
- Eventually, all religions will come together and merge into one perfect way to worship God.
- The devil has horns and a goatee; God has a full, gray beard, being very old.
- Peace is best achieved by having better weapons than the opposition.
- Wars are fought for freedom and democracy, to improve our lives, never for the earth's resources.
- Science will eventually make us healthier, happier, live longer and feel secure. Science will also see to it that the polluted environment will be cleaned up. The air, the water and the soil will be pure again, the way the Creator had intended.
- We should trust our political and religious leaders to achieve lasting peace. God will guide them until they get it right.
- Democracy will be able to unite all the warring nations,

- making the world one big happy family, with wars a thing of the past. The United Nations will be a great help here.
- Corruption, at all levels, will be done away with, forever. Just wait.
- Democracy will persuade Imams, the Muslims' religious leaders, to stop telling their flock that women are cattle.
- Muslim leaders will also declare that killing infidels is not okay.
- They will no longer proclaim that having intercourse with little boys and girls, or with camels, is all right.
- But prayers of those who still continue this habit will not be answered until they have washed afterward, at least up to their elbows.
- Science will discover the secret of life, and perhaps give us immortality.
- Nothing ever changes. Things are today what they were yesterday, or six thousand years ago. People have always lived to be a hundred, give or take a few years, and that people at one time lived to be nine hundred-plus is suspect. That eternal life existed earlier is definitely a figment of the imagination.
- "The end of the world" is not the end of the *World*. Instead, the Creator will totally destroy his beautiful creation, our *planet*, with us on it. This is the same God who is all love, ever-forgiving, who won't kill anybody. It is hard to understand why he would do such a terrible thing.

Read the list again, and when you're done, what do you now think "sin" is? And who is the Devil?

Committing Original Sin was a three-fold process, religious, political and commercial, in the order of lethal severity. The Creator wanted to fill the earth with living souls, who would appreciate what he had done for them. However, the renegade angel Lucifer (Satan, if you wish) worked on our vanity and our arrogance and sense of self-importance, and promised us progress, prosperity, peace and an opportunity to *be like gods* if we followed *his* lead.

Our forebears had a choice: to either stay with the Creator and live, or throw in their lot with the Great Opposer and Misleader, learning about Good and Evil, and become like gods in the process. They consciously chose Lucifer. This cost us our right to life, and we were handed the "going-to-heaven-and-seeing-God" doctrine in exchange. This was the *religious*, most deadly part of Original Sin.

The result of the *political* part, the second most deadly, we can see all around us. When we read the story of the Tower of Babel, we learn that the Creator does not favor heavy concentrations of people in one place. He knew that building strongholds such as Babel would eventually lead to cities, after that to independent nations, who would be warring with one another, with ever-increasing violence to people as well as to the environment. By following Lucifer's lead, the World has done exactly that. We now know the added consequences thereof: overpopulation with its attendant poisoning of air, water and soil, and having to deal with deadly, unstoppable diseases. We have eaten the fruits of the Tree of the Knowledge of Good and Evil. Now we know what they taste like.

The *commercial* part is the least deadly of the three. But, although Money became a necessary evil as trade between the various nations increased, it can quickly turn into a god, with its own temple-like buildings, as we now well know.

Knowing all this, each individual has a choice: Either embrace the World with its Religions, its divisive politics, and its financial arrangements, or acknowledge that it is leading nowhere but to self-destruction. Either recognize the Devil and still join in, or ignore him and his perishable World.

The truth sets free. Recognizing what or who the Devil is produces a sense of relief. One doesn't have to be afraid anymore of something that does not exist, like a monster in a bad dream, or feel guilty about individual misdeeds which one may or may not have committed against some angry Deity. The monster has been exposed, and he is *us*, ruling the World the way we do.

Sin is our group activity.

Why does the Devil do this?

Satan is well aware of the Creator's plan to fill the earth with living souls, because the plan still exists. What Satan, embodying the opposition, does not want is a World he has no hold over. That's why he is trying to prevent anyone from recognizing the truth about him. His objective is to deny the Creator as many subjects as possible, even if he thought it necessary to kill all of the World's population.

And that is where his plan will fail. Even if one percent of the seven and a half billion people now on earth turn its back on him, he loses.

Whether the foregoing is true is for each person to decide individually. No-one can make up someone else's mind about this. Coercion leads nowhere.

Violence

Violence is not necessarily restricted to wars or acts committed between individual people. It could also be violence to the environment or to the rules of Yahweh. For example, the fact that we think agriculture is necessary does not mean that it is approved by Yahweh. If we realize that grand-scale agriculture is one of the causes of overpopulation and its consequences, we may come to see it as violence to the environment.

Violence to the rules of Yahweh is mentioned in Genesis 6: The time came when the sons of the true God (the offspring of Adam and Eve) took wives from the indigenous population, which produced violent hybrid beings called Nephilim. One of those was Lamech, a descendant of Cain. This way of life constituted violence to the rule not to have anything to do with the existing population, and certainly not sexually.

Violence to the environment became evident when, after about two hundred years, the ground in Southern Mesopotamia became so salinized because of the continuous use of irrigation and possibly fertilizer that certain crops could not be grown there anymore. It became necessary to abandon some cities and build new ones farther north.

Jesus the redeemer

As in the case of Noah, Abraham and Moses, there is no solid evidence that the Redeemer, the man Jesus, as described in the gospels of Matthew, Mark, Luke and John, was an historical figure. It has been established that Mark was the first disciple to write about him, but there is controversy about whether he was the only one doing the writing.

The book of Mark is thought to be an artificial and theological construct bearing little relationship to Jesus' actual life. Some of the writing is attributed to a number of Mark's co-workers.

The other gospel writers, Matthew and Luke, apparently borrowed heavily from the Mark text, and possibly also from a document called *The Q Source*.

Other sources of information about Jesus

Primary sources other than those in the Book are Tacitus and Flavius Josephus. Tacitus was a Roman historian, who mentioned Chrestians, or Christians, in relation to the burning of Rome.

The emperor Nero, who was suspected of instigating the fire, indignantly put the blame on those abominable Christians, who ate their God and drank his blood, a practice close to cannibalism.

Flavius Josephus, who in the year 93 A.D. published a lengthy history of the Jews, the *Testimonium Flavianum*, which included a reference to Jesus, as being a wise man, even the Messiah, who performed surprising deeds. The wise man had subsequently been condemned by Pontius Pilate, a Roman procurator, who had him executed.

It would seem that this had enough historical value to be taken as confirmation that Jesus had existed. However, critics of this manuscript claim that this could not have been written by a Jewish man—it sounded too Christian. They suggest that the paragraph dealing with Jesus being the Messiah was not authentic, and was added later by Christian copyists, probably in the third or fourth century.

Whether any of this has historical value may not be important. There is a strong possibility that the real Jesus in prophecy is not the single person who was walking the earth at the time he did, but the symbol for a much longer-range prediction (six thousand years from the World's beginning) of a grouping of people appearing at the time of the end.

This collection of persons, consisting of individuals from all nations, would, like Jesus, denounce the World's violent Governments and its fake Organized Religions, putting its collective faith in a different political setup with loftier principles—a peaceful group that would rely on divine intervention and not succumb to the temptation to take matters into its own hands, most definitely not by military means.

Seen in this light, the Good News Story makes more sense. Now, in the first half of the 21st century, it is apparent to many people that the World is on a self-perpetuating path of self-destruction, with nobody in charge powerful enough to make meaningful changes to its downward spiral. It seems that the time for this prophecy has come.

Jesus, the story

In the King James Translation, the book of John starts with: In the beginning was the Word, and the Word was with God, and the Word was God. The same was in the beginning with God.

It makes little sense to make us believe that God was God and also with God. Other translations make it somewhat clearer.

The New World Translation, published by the Watchtower Bible Society, states: In the beginning the Word was, and the Word was with God and the Word was *a god*. This one was in the beginning with God.

The Word was the *man* Jesus. "The Word became flesh and walked among us," John put it (1:14). It shows that Jesus, when on earth, was not "the God," but "a god," a man. Organized Religion wants us to accept the idea that The God came down to earth (from where?) *in person* and let himself be killed by the very men he created. If you want to believe that, go ahead. One is free to believe anything.

That's why John called him: *The Word*. Verse 3 says: "All things came into existence through him and not even one thing came into existence without him," in effect stating that he was billions of years old, and had been instrumental in the creating process. He might have been God's only actual creation (only-begotten son, 3:16), who then proceeded to create everything his "Father" commanded him to create.

Taking this a step further, the conclusion may be drawn that the spoken word is more powerful than anything else. That's why it is important to listen to the things he *said*, rather than concentrate on the things he *did*, such as the miracles he performed.

Whether he performed miracles at all, and how, is hard to say. Some of the performances seem contrary to human experience and therefore beyond the realm of possibilities. On the other hand, we do not really know what the brain is capable of.

It appears that he had acquired instruction, knowledge and understanding to a degree not known to us. At a certain juncture in his earthly life he must have come to the realization that he may be a forerunner of the ultimate Redeemer mentioned in Genesis.

He was not of this world. It does not mean that he came from another planet. It means, if we interpret the Book correctly, that he was unwilling to participate in the World's political setup. He would be considered an insubordinate rebel today, because he vigorously denounced the establishment, and certainly its religious institutions. Religion portrays him as a pious softy, a man of sorrows, the founder of modern Christianity, but that is definitely not the case. Like Adam, he could have succumbed to the machinations of his own mind and given in to the temptations the world presented. He was human, and very well capable of "sinning."

Consider the temptation

In Matthew 4:1-11 we read that he was "in the wilderness" for forty days without food, and that he became hungry. However, this is symbolism, a story, like many others in the Book.

Medical science tells us that it is absolutely impossible to survive that long without food. After three weeks his body would have begun "mining" the muscles and vital organs for energy, and loss of bone marrow would have become life-threatening. Within forty days his body would have deteriorated to the point of dying, and no amount of food would have restored his health.

Wilderness metaphor

The narration says he was in the wilderness "in the spirit." It means he was not in an actual wilderness. He may have been at home, or out walking, and letting his thoughts have a free rein. Neither was he without regular food. However, he was without "bread," the symbol for proper information from the right source. "Wilderness" was a metaphor for the World he found himself in, and for a month and a half Jesus was thinking about his options to change it for the better, like many who made an attempt earlier and many who gave it a try after him. He may have been approached by some who saw in him the potential for exceptional leadership.

The stones in the story represented the unpalatable dogmas the world presents. Could he change them into "bread"—useful information? After forty days he decided he could not; it would be the end of him. He kept thinking the right thoughts, thereby defying "Satan," a metaphor for his human inclination to follow the impulse to create a world by himself, like Adam did. He stopped thinking along those lines before it had a chance to overpower his brain and kill him.

He could have become a great world leader or an influential Rabbi then and there had he agreed to comply with the World's requirements. He was a man, like Adam. To see him as a god incapable of bad thoughts denies him his victory: as a human being he did not let his brain be contaminated by the World.

Instead he began to tell people that *The God* had promised a new kind of political system on earth. This system would not come about by human hands. He called it the Kingdom of Heaven (Matthew 4:17)—not a kingdom *in* heaven, but *of* heaven, with eternal life *on earth* for its citizens. A system ruled by heavenly, loftier principles, not by the standards of the present world. And he, Jesus, was not going to interfere with that plan, as Adam had done.

He vigorously denounced the religious leaders of his day, calling them vipers, hypocrites, blind guides and whitewashed graves, good looking on the outside, but full of decay within (Matthew 5:20, 6:1-5 and 23:13 and 23:27).

Prayer had a special purpose and was to be done *inside the house, in private,* not on street corners, where others could see and admire the supplicant (Matthew 6:5). He explained the reason for prayer. Compare the way it is written in the Bible (Matthew 5:9) with the following down-to-earth version which I propose:

Our most perfect Father, we want your Name to be recognized. We want your government to be installed on earth and your perfect laws implemented. Supply us with the food of learning ("bread") every day and forgive us if we make a mistake (in declaring you), the same way we forgive those who commit a mistake involving us. Let us not be tempted (by the world), but get rid of the Evil One (Satan) for us (basically, change our evil inclination by instructing us).

Killed by Religion

This kind of prayer, if understood the way it was meant, does not sit well with those in power. They love the system as it is and look askance at anyone arguing against it, as Jesus did. Its religious branch, too, was fearful to see its high pedestal reviled and perhaps removed, and it went after Jesus with a vengeance. They accused him of insurrection against the (Roman) establishment, and demanded his execution.

He was condemned by a reluctant Roman officer, tortured and killed according to Roman military protocol. This involved humiliation, flogging and execution by nailing the body to what was probably a stake, a tree, or, less likely, a cross.[5] It is well to realize that this was by command of the *religious leaders* of his day.

According to the Book he was resurrected on the third day after his murder, appeared to a number of people, after which he went to heaven. This needs some clarification.

Heaven is not a place where people, or even angels, go. Nobody goes to heaven. He was not lifted up to disappear into the clouds. Mythology played a heavy role here. Many of his disciples were simple men, brought up in the ways of the world. Some thought that he was the Son of God. Since God was sup-

---

[5] A wooden cross is not a simple thing to make. If you have ever tried to construct one, you will know that it involves fairly precise chiseling in order for the two parts to fit together. It is doubtful that the Romans would go to that kind of extra trouble to execute their criminals. They simply nailed the culprit to a tree or what you would now call a telephone pole, put it upright in the ground, publicly displaying the dying criminal as a warning to potential miscreants.

posed to be in heaven, and heaven being above the clouds, the natural way of thinking was for him to go "up."

It is not likely that the gospel writers were ignorant of the fact that "the heavens" was a metaphor for excellence, and was most definitely not referring to a "place." "Jesus went to heaven" can only have meant one thing: he had passed the test eventually required from every human being. He had displayed the right spirit.

By dying while his brain was uncontaminated he was now "at the right hand of God." He had conquered death and was therefore in a position to grant eternal life to others. He had shown that he could be trusted to establish Yahweh's government on earth. Satan would be neutralized when that happened and later killed.

He promised to return when the time was ripe. However, understand that he will not return as a person, but as the invisible head of his new government.

The need for damage control

Whether it really happened or not, the Book relates the story of Jesus, "the last Adam" (1 Cor 15:4), who appeared on earth to announce a drastic change in the world's political and religious setup. For his efforts he was killed by the Roman government at the request of the religious authorities.

He had been mentioned before, even as far back as the beginning of Genesis, as the man (a "seed") who would take over from the first Adam, who had failed in his mission and lost his (and our) right to life. He would redeem us from acquired death by completing Adam's mission and be killed in the process.

However, fact or fiction, spokesmen of Organized Religion would rather you didn't find out who was responsible for his reported killing, preferring to make the Roman Authority the guilty party, suggesting Jesus was executed for insurrection, being a rebel, a danger to the Occupation.

But there was a problem. Some of the things Jesus said and did, or may have said and done, had been written up by various individuals some years after his death, painting a damaging picture of Organized Religion and its leaders, which he had called poisonous snakes, whitewashed graves and more, accusing them of grossly misleading people. The same records also noted who his *real killers* were.

Damage control was definitely indicated. What could be better than to shift attention from the day of his *death* to that of his *birth*, and make it coincide with the heathen festival of the return of the sun after winter? Pagan people were used to some kind of celebration at the end of December.

The early Christians put more weight on Easter, and the time and manner of his death. The day of one's birth was thought to be of less consequence than the day of one's demise. The state of the dying person's mind as regards to his relations with The God at the time of his death was what counted. However, Organized Religion was not to be deterred.

The fact that they were his murderers necessitated that they divert the attention from Easter as the main remembrance ritual. Forget the *purpose* of Jesus' death. They would deal with that later. The emphasis at Easter could perhaps be put on rabbits, eggs, special hats for the women.

Hence *Christmas.*

Christmas is the ideal form of damage control. The feeling of goodwill toward all men is represented in the festive sound of carols with their peace-on-earth theme, the illuminated evergreen trees with their glittering ornaments, the special foodstuffs, the spirit of giving, the holiday greetings, the days off from work, all directed to create an atmosphere of well-being, warmth and happiness. Good for business, too. Not only that, but it is clear that God is on our side. All is well with the world. Hey! See how we use the name of Christ, his Son, everywhere? Christmas cards, Christmas trees, Christmas cheer, Christmas lights. We are all Christians, practically the world over. Europe, North America, Australia, all followers of Christ. Just too bad the Romans had to kill him; he was such a good man, such a good teacher. But what can you expect from pagans such as the Romans?

To see how the minds of the leaders of Organized Religion work, consider this: The Book indicates that *Jesus was not born on December 25;* no one is quite certain what the actual date was. The fact that the book reports that sheepherders were out in the open at night makes it unlikely that it took place in December, in the dead of winter. But December is the time of year the sun "turns north" again (actually on December 21, the winter solstice). December 25 was the date of a pagan festival in Rome, *"natalis solis invicti"* (the birthday of the unconquered sun), chosen in A.D. 274 by the emperor Aurelius, because on that day an increase of light begins to show. (Both Aurelius and Constantine were sun worshippers.) Houses were decorated with greenery and lights, presents given to children and the poor. *Both Christmas and Epiphany, twelve days later, on January 6, are transformations of pagan celebrations of the winter solstice.*

Canaanites believed that their god of fertility and cattle, Baal, was reborn in December after dying at the end of the harvesting season.

This may be why the Emperor Constantine the Great, a sun worshipper to the end, who claimed to be reborn as a Christian in the fourth century, set, at his mother's suggestion, December 25 as Christmas, it being the ideal birth day for Christ. (Emperor Constantine was the one who saw a cross in the sky with the motto: "under this sign you will conquer," and conquer was what he wanted.) Using the December 25 date was thought, correctly as it turned out, to help pagans all over the known world to convert to Christianity, while keeping their pagan holidays, as for example the *Saturnalia* (December 17-24), a time of merry-making and exchange of presents in the pagan Roman world.

The Christmas tree is not an accident either. Tree worship has been a pagan tradition for as long as Organized Religion has existed. Trees were believed to be manifestations or symbols of supernatural power, and made into objects of worship. The use of evergreens, a symbol of survival, in modern Christmas observances was a way to integrate a form of paganism into Christianity, so as not to alienate the masses, who are generally slow to adopt new and different ways of worship. The Teutonic races also used trees in the great midwinter festival, Yule, held in late December.

So, all is well with the world? Absolutely! Organized Religion can relax. People do not necessarily think of the cruel manner of his death anymore when Christmas rolls around. The attention is on the presents, the tree and its ornaments, the endless Christmas carols on radio and television, the special dinners and cakes. The control is absolute, it is thought.

Making Jesus into God was also a clever diversion. By doing this, they hid the fact that he was *human* at the time he was murdered. Gods *cannot* sin. So, if he was superhuman, what was so special about his accomplishment? All we have here is a god coming down to earth to give us a new, better kind of religion. A teacher of sorts. His death as a criminal had nothing to do with us. It blacked out the real reason for his coming: to counteract what Adam had done. Not as a God, but *as a human being*, thereby obtaining power over death itself. Not as a "Great Teacher," but to be killed for the harsh words he spoke against the World's violent and godless, "wicked" way of governing, and certainly to expose the supporting role the religious leaders of his (and our) day played and play in it.

Organized Religion will be with us until the end of the World, of which it is such an integral part—a world of division, corruption, violence and greed. The World *needs* Organized Religion. It could not exist without it. Similarly, Organized Religion would not last another day without the world in its present form. The World and its present Religious setup are soul mates.

The Book of Revelation, the Apocalypse

Our world is less than perfect, as anyone would agree. It is one of illusions—illusions of power, illusions of wealth, illusions of worship. It is ruled by human traits: arrogance, ignorance, violence, greed, dishonesty, ineptitude and even criminality. These traits, taken together, constitute Satan, or the Antichrist. "He" has been with us for thousands of years, and when the Book speaks of the *End of the World*, it means that "his" world will be terminated and replaced by another, peaceful, more enlightened one.

Misinformation

For obvious reasons there is not one government of any nation on earth ever to let us know that this possibility exists. The acknowledgment would reflect unfavorably on its reign, and in effect predict its own downfall. Their propaganda, therefore, prefers to divert our attention away from this prediction by misinforming and frightening us by liberally exchanging "earth" for "world," thereby making its own prediction: the likelihood of the destruction of the planet by a vengeful God who is angry with us. Its Organized Religion branch is very helpful here by doing most of the misinforming. *Misleading is Religion's main function.*

Revelation, or the Apocalypse, written in the years 81-96 A.D., is an exposé, a revealing, an uncovering, a lifting of the veil. It is meant to explain to the reader that Religion is synonymous with "The Whore of Babylon," who "fornicates" with the present inadequate system of Government (the nations). Although this unveiling seems to suggest actual violence and destruction, remember that these are images that symbolically describe and highlight events leading to the end of the World's *system*, not the end of the planet itself. Even the word "apocalypse," which means "exposé," has now, because of official misinformation, become synonymous with "calamity" in the public eye. The role of Government and Religion in this matter is unmistakable.

666

The Book informs us that 666 is the number of a man—a *human being*. There is no doubt that it pertains to the political system, and the oppressive grip it has on the world. In Hebrew numerology, the number 6 stands for "imperfection," and the number 10 for "wholeness," as if to say, something totally inadequate. Six, six times 10, and six times 10 times 10 indicates that the Book considers everything in the System lacking. With its monetary, commercial, governmental and religious components, what it calls "the Beast" is found wanting and will be brought to an end.

The human condition deals with money, consumerism, government and religion. One by one these will fall. John's vision in chapter 6 of Revelation includes a description of either rampant inflation or a terrible food shortage, or both. Famine, diseases and death are mentioned. In chapter 18, the "kings" of the earth weep and beat themselves because of the failure of what they considered a great situation. The "traveling merchants" lament that their customers have disappeared. It paints a picture of the end of the good times and the shameless wealth they enjoyed while the Beast was in power.

Religion will fall last. There will come a time when people, and even the Beast itself, will turn against the false beliefs and devastate that part of the organization. Exactly when that will take place, no-one knows. We should, however, keep our attention focused on events that are likely to lead to a possible big change in religious perception.

When all these things happen, the world's population will probably be astonished, because no earthly power has ever managed to change the ways of the World.

For example, it looks as if we are now, in 2015, experiencing a severe world-wide meltdown of the monetary system. If this be the beginning of the final chapter of the present world's powerbase, we might also soon be experiencing the demise of the world's commercial system and after that the collapse of the Government/Religion combo.

Money and the commercial system

Normally, we trust banks to keep our earnings safe and have the money ready when we need it—to buy a house, or a car, or pay for our kids' college education. This works well as long as banks can be relied on to make the right decisions, and to not betray our trust by solely having their own welfare at heart. But when the elements of greed and criminality are injected into the system, it is not surprising that things go awry.

In the beginning of the 21st century a handful of callous traders, employed in high positions by certain banks, managed to severely damage the monetary system by treating money as a commodity that could be created at will.

They created trillions and trillions of so-called "Gilt-edged Securities" that proved to be worthless. These securities were traded world-wide. Ignorant (and perhaps unwilling) Government had failed to realize that Banks could not be trusted to police themselves and were suddenly presented with an ocean of imaginary money in October 2008.

As the story unfolded it became apparent that some of this fake money was, in effect, the principal foundation of some big-name financial companies' wealth. The illusion of wealth became apparent.

Consequently, a number of large banks failed, halting the supply of commercial loans, causing many businesses to fold. As a result millions of people were thrown out of work all over the world. One whole nation—Iceland—went bankrupt. Government, in an attempt to stem the tide, is now scrambling to turn imaginary money into real money by "printing" and handing out billions to the guilty parties. It is not at all sure whether this strategy will work. It may turn out to be the illusion of a solution. However, the attempt is still quietly, almost secretly, being pursued.

In order to survive, the commercial system depends on the willingness of customers to buy its products. However, the millions of their clients, all over the globe, who are now without an adequate income have become cautious and are putting off buying items they can do without. The system sees its income base eroding and perhaps slipping away for some time to come. Many businesses have failed and may never recover. It could indeed be the end of the commercial system as we know it. It is therefore possible that, as John predicts in Revelation 18:10, "The merchants will weep."

The problem may sometimes seem to be solved because the Stock Market is going up, but the Stock Market is not a reliable indicator of the strength or weakness of the monetary situation.

The Government/Religion combination

The main task of Government's religion-department is to help hide the truth about the origin and nature of Sin. The government arrangement in the world we know is basically an inept and arrogant management idea, and it uses religion to cover up the fact that its rulers are incapable of ruling effectively. That is why Religion piously claims that there is a great mystery going on, a mystery so deep that it cannot be understood by the common person.

The Book must therefore be interpreted by members of their clergy, who in a mysterious way know more about God than most other individuals. This leaves ample opportunity for obfuscation and cover-up. This is more apparent in some countries than others. Religion plays much less of a role in Western Europe than in the United States or the Middle East, for example.

However, the truth is not at all mysterious and is really very simple. The Book explains that Yahweh, who made the universe and its rules and laws, knows that ignoring his universal laws and breaking his rules—sin —leads to an unwanted course of events that may take thousands of years to undo. The wish for world domination has resulted in an amalgamation of living conditions—shopping malls, money-dispensing machines, television with global programming, cell phones and virtually identical weapons of war.

The wrong way of governing people involved single-crop farming, city-building and general misuse of the earth's resources. Such action inevitably led to nation-building, empire building and wars between nations. It led to overpopulation, with its problems of pollution and poisoning of the environment, world-wide hunger and incurable diseases. That is why Yahweh warned Adam and Eve to stay away from "the fruit of *that* tree" (of the knowledge of good and evil).

One of the ploys used by Religion to steer the attention away from these truths is to suggest that Sin is somehow synonymous with *Sex*. Many Americans may remember the tear-streaked televangelist declaring: "I have sinned, my Lord!" referring to his inability to control his sexual impulses. However, he was wrong here as well. Of course he had sinned, but his sin was his inability to recognize that the 666 syndrome is the actual God of his World, and that the God he was talking to is known in the Book as the Beast.

Because of the constant, identical propaganda of the media throughout the world, billions of people never doubt the veracity of what they hear. It is indeed hard to accept that information being broadcast in practically every country on the planet could be engineered to be misleading. The way of the World has become accepted truth, especially when enforced by the clergy of whatever denomination. Opposition to the customary view is seen as subversive, disloyal, unpatriotic and even blasphemous.

The status quo is a safe haven for those who prefer to go with the flow rather than to give the matter a second thought. The violence, the pollution, the poisonous environment, the diseases, the hunger, the inequality are accepted by them as the normal. The phenomena are perceived as the growing pains of an evolving world community on its way to a peaceful existence.

However, to trust the powers-that-be to bring this Utopia about will prove to be like betting on the wrong horse; an ideal that will never come true that way. It is far more probable that the course taken six thousand years ago will end in a tremendous disaster. Then we will have learned that there is a difference between good and bad. No doubt Eve's "eating" will then come to mind.

In summing up, it is clear that the choice of getting away from Fake Religion and Government influence is an individual decision. It can never be imposed on anyone. Matthew 11:25 states: "The truth is hidden from the wise and intellectual ones and revealed to [depending on the translation] babes, infants or little children."

Government or no government

Can we do without government? It is a question that has several answers, depending on what one means by the term. The way the world is run nowadays, one could easily come to the conclusion that we would be better off without government. However, the way of the violent world is the result of thousands of years of self-indulgence, driven by greed, arrogance, stupidity and a misplaced sense of self-importance. If only one of those traits could be eliminated, everyone, including the rulers, would already be better off.

From the rulers' point of view it probably began with a genuine wish to assist nomads, making life easier for them with organized food production, protecting them from other tribes' raids, perhaps even hoping to curb the violent streak in the general population. But it did not take long for the rulers to find out that their assistance was only marginally necessary and not always appreciated. Nevertheless, they persisted, and attempted to combine other areas under their influence, in the mistaken idea that a peaceful situation would follow if the rest of the known world were subjected to a one-man rule where violence was outlawed. It did not turn out that way, of course. Other rulers also thought of themselves as capable of reaching the same peaceful Utopia, but with themselves in the leading role.

Being a ruler meant to be looked up to, and had several other perks, like wealth and ease of living, often in seclusion. Strife ensued, first between tribal rulers, then between those who built cities, which resulted in city states and later countries, nations. The quest for peace became a matter of having a well-equipped army, preventatively warding off a perceived enemy, or of making the enemy see the advantage of agreeing to the suggestions of the stronger ruler. It became the accepted way of government. Nothing much has changed over the past six thousand years.

Generations that followed, not familiar with the life of nomads, became used to living in organized communities, and many, in due course, most likely preferred the new lifestyle. The result was a general acceptance of the necessity of government, no doubt influenced by the accompanying propaganda from the ruling clan. It became accepted wisdom that without leadership society could not function properly. Violence was an unfortunate but inevitable part of it: a means to an end. The rulers did not discourage this way of thinking—realizing that the violent streak in people could be used to advantage in their army recruitment.

The king, or lugal, became a revered person, sometimes perceived as a god, or a son of a god, and later, when such a claim could no longer be sustained, the representative of a particular deity. As a rule, leaders in the past were not chosen. They were either self-appointed or the result of misplaced awe for, and confidence in, an individual because of his accumulated wealth. For all practical purposes they were dictators. The problem with this mindset is that persons in such a position are bound to lose touch with reality and smugly think of themselves and their family as invincible and omnipotent.

Democracy changed a little of that. It gave some power into the hands of ordinary citizens, allowing them to choose a particular leader. It is open to debate if this produced a meaningful improvement in the way government operates. The man in the street is not necessarily mentally equipped to know what is good for him, or for society. He can easily be swayed by unrealistic promises or by a wicked demonization process. Sometimes the candidates are mediocre, or are influenced by money from interests other than those of the voter or general population—even money from another nation.

Managing the World becomes more complex with population increase, which in itself is the result of mismanagement and over-confidence. It is difficult to meaningfully change course after such a long time of set behavior. The main obstacle to change is thousands of years of conditioning. More realistic approaches are often seen as weak or irrelevant if they tilt toward a government style where less narcissistic values are prevalent and where might is not synonymous with right.

A leader who favors appeasement may soon be labeled weak and indecisive if he does not want to adhere to the domineering syndrome. The opposing party will use this to discredit the candidate, causing his or her election or re-election to hang in the balance.

The foregoing makes it seem as though all governments are evil or wicked, or even that such epithets apply in most cases. Be assured that there have been governments led by benign dictators who had nothing but the welfare of their constituents at heart. Hammurabi, Napoleon and others come to mind, instituting laws that gave certain rights and access to protection for ordinary citizens unheard of in a period of time when the whims of absolute rulers constituted the law of the land. Some of the laws they enacted are still in force.

Is government necessary? Are armed forces necessary? What are we to do if the enemy insists on perpetrating violent acts toward the country you happen to live in? Isn't it better to meet violence with violence? There are no easy answers for that, as World War II has shown. Adolf Hitler's decadent Nazi organization was designed to take over the world, but was stopped by those who are now in charge of a great portion of it. It was a violent, bloody confrontation that caused disruption on a huge scale. Was it necessary?

First of all we have to consider that wars are not conducted by the citizens of a country. They do the fighting, but the decision to fight is made by rulers. Leader against leader. It is doubtful that one community would attack another without a reasonable cause. "Enemy" is a relative term. International enmity must be cultivated and maintained, almost daily. The Christmas celebration on the battlefield in the last year of World War I has made that very clear. The leaders of both sides were not happy with the expression of brotherhood that took place in the trenches. It damaged morale; the fighting spirit had been attacked. The enemy suddenly was less of an enemy, maybe even a friend This unwanted state of affairs had to be brought to an end as soon as possible, before it got out of hand. The bloody slaughter was ordered to resume the next day and went on to the bitter end.

The defeat of the Germans in World War I and the humiliation that followed in 1918 is a good example of a long-term enmity that can be cultivated by a determined leader. World War II was nothing more than a continuation of World War I. The twenty years in between were a period of relative, and sometimes uneasy, rest.

The Crusades

But even acts committed hundreds of years previous are often vividly remembered, certainly if Religion is involved.

The Crusades were a series of so-called defensive religious military campaigns, started in the year 1095 by the Holy Roman Catholic Church under Pope Urban II and ended in 1291. Muslims were living close to the border with Europe and expanding their religious and political influence. Urban wanted to stop the upmarch, retake Palestine and make Jerusalem a Christian city. He forgave all sins for those who joined the war effort.

Maybe he should not have said that, although he must have impressed many of the participants with his substantial celestial power. Maybe Urban, in his zeal, assumed that the soldiers on this particular Holy mission were sufficiently imbued with the Holy Spirit to transform them into saints as they took up the sword. It didn't turn out that way. Matthew 9:5 must have come to mind. The Crusaders, as they became known, committed many atrocities during the two centuries the conflict lasted. They may have been under the impression that forgiveness of their sins included those they might commit in the future as well. Because of their behavior the schism between Christianity and Islam was permanently widened, and Christians, who until that time had been allowed to live peacefully in Islam communities, free to practice their religion unhindered, were from then on persecuted and went into decline.

In spite of the clout he thought he had with his Deity, Urban did not succeed in retaking the holy land. The Holy Roman Catholic Church had to admit defeat in 1291. The reverberations of the campaigns are felt to this day.

Exact figures of the casualties in the two-hundred-year-long conflict are not known, but it is estimated to be in the hundreds of thousands, maybe even millions, most of them Christians. Many more Jews and Christians were killed than Muslims, many of them innocent bystanders. The City of Constantinople was looted in the Fourth Crusade in 1204. It meant the end of the Byzantine Empire. Asia was converted wholesale to Islam. All the events can be labeled Fruits of Eden.

Although the Church was not a country and Pope Urban was not officially a political leader, it is clear that actions taken a thousand years ago can still have an adverse effect on the news of today. We deal with them in the everyday newscasts from the Middle East.

Government or no government? The short conclusion is that some form of leadership is needed, but that the aspiring leaders should go back to school, learn from history to be humbler, and when they enter the classroom be told to leave their swords at home, together with their egos.

The newest invention—the Rapture

The inventors of religious myth, well aware of the confusion around the "end-of-the-world" scenario, have not long ago added a new dimension to this misinformation: *the Rapture!* There are people, they say, who will be spared this violent end. Moments before the planet is destroyed, God saves all the Flumbees. He takes all the *First Lutheran Methodical Baptistarian Evangelists*, the FLUMBEES, as they are about their normal daily business, and whisks them away, not a moment to soon, to heaven. (These inventors are cousins of the Masters of Ceremony who generously give suicide car-bombers seventy-seven perpetual virgins on their arrival in Paradise.)

One is bound to ask: what happens to an Escalade SUV, in cruise control at 70 miles per hour, when the driver, a Flumbee, is suddenly taken to heaven, rendering the car driverless? Would it not be reasonable to expect that the vehicle would go out of control and hit, say, a car with innocent women and children, killing them all? Of course, as with everything else, there is a catch.

Because there *are* no innocent victims! Since they are not Flumbees they are all guilty! Heaven is for Flumbees only, you see. They are the true believers. They have been converted from deep sin to being all good. They no longer swear or lust after their neighbors' wives; they no longer molest their children or even talk to them in a derogatory way. They no longer exceed the speed limit. They no longer cheat on their taxes but pay whatever the government asks, uncomplaining and on time. They are good to their fellow-citizens, even to non-Flumbees. You could say they have become perfect heavenly souls, obeying all the rules!

To be sure, there is no reason to fear that heaven will become overcrowded; it is obvious that there are only very few who qualify.

Like much of Religion's belief, or irreversible dogma, the Rapture is based on information accidentally or deliberately applied to mislead. None of this would have been necessary if the Original Myth of immediately going to heaven after death, or even when still alive, as in the Rapture case, had not been introduced in the first place. However, once one has said "A," one must also say "B."

There is a parallel with staging a war on the pretext that the enemy possesses weapons of mass destruction and wants to use them to harm your country. Once you have made such an official statement, even after it was later known to be based on deliberate and consciously fabricated "information," it is very hard to confess that a "mistake" has been made.

The mythical Rapture hinges on the idea that the world and the earth are one and the same thing. There would not be a Rapture if there were no confusion as to what was what. Be assured that there is no need to be afraid. The Book wants all peace-loving men of goodwill to understand that the earth is not going to be harmed. What is coming to an end is the way we *do* things on earth. Our "general affairs of life" will undergo a drastic change. The Rapture will never take place. *Guaranteed!* It is a myth, like practically all the other fiction Organized Religion has come up with.

Religion

Mind like Parachute—only work when open.—Charlie Chan

Contrary to what many people still firmly believe, the Book is not a morality manual. Although there is a certain common-sense amount of warning about bad behavior, like stealing, killing, lying for gain and profit, that is not the main message. Instead, the Bible is a *political* document, which focuses on the present violent system of governments on our earth and its coming replacement, still on the same earth, by a rulership led by loftier principles. In addition, it points out who the real God is, lets us know the name of the world's pseudo god and warns us about worshipping such a false god and the consequences thereof.

From the first pages of Genesis to the final pages of Revelations, covering six thousand years, the Book tells us about the hijacking of the legitimate government and the several attempts at world domination. One try after another has ended in defeat. Egypt, Assyria, Babylon, Medo-Persia, Greece and Rome all tried and failed. The Book describes the final throes of the system, with the diseases, the lawlessness, the violence, the hunger and the climate changes, the sudden collapse when it seems that everything is going swimmingly (1 Thess 5:2-4, Matt 25:13, Rev 16:15, Luke 12:39).

Government does not want us to hear about this and uses Religion and sundry other methods to steer us away from the message. One of the methods used is to play word games with our minds; make untrue suggestions—lies—designed to twist the meaning of the things we read and thereby thoroughly confusing us. They can take a statement, turn it upside down as well as back to front and inside out until its true meaning is unrecognizable. Then, sanctimoniously, it is dished up as the truth, the whole truth and nothing but. No wonder we have concluded that there is something wrong with the *Book,* never suspecting that those we trust to do the right thing, brokering the Truth for us, have bamboozled us on a grand scale.

Religion's suggestions and "explanations" have a habit of making us feel uncomfortable about ourselves, guilty and somewhat afraid to offend the "Lord," because of possible consequences. That, of course, is the very purpose, to condition us and accept the official plans and schemes meekly and blindly.

One telling example: In most Bibles, including the version placed in hotel rooms by the Mormons, the sentence "Deliver us from *the Evil One*" in Jesus' prayer suggestion (Matthew 6:5-13, Luke 11:1-4, KJT) clearly referring to Satan, has purposefully been changed to "Deliver us from *evil.*"

Organized Religion prefers to steer the attention away from their god, thereby putting the burden on *us,* as though "evil" must be understood as an unavoidable part of our make-up, as if it would have to be exorcized. Even the regular King James Version renders it as such, but the *New International Version,* the *English Revised Version, the New World Translation* and the *International Standard Version* now use "The Evil One."

One more reason to conclude that the Book is the natural enemy of Religion as well as Government and is, in their opinion, in need of adjustment and editing to better fit the official view.

And then there is the physical and mental cruelty that sometimes characterizes Religion itself.

The Inquisition

In late medieval days, from the 12th century until the early 1800's, the Inquisition was a means of assuring that members of the Holy Roman Church did not succumb to *heresy,* or evil viewpoints (other than those of the Church's dogmas). This was not so much for the correction and the good of the accused individual's soul, but for the "public good."

Once a person's guilt of the religious crime of heresy had been established, he or she was put in the hands of a secular magistrate, who decided on the type of punishment, which differed by local law. It could vary between being burned alive at the stake, imprisonment for life, banishment, or confiscation of properties of those over a certain income.

Pope Innocent IV, in 1252, decided that the use of torture to elicit confessions was not only allowed, but preferred, and by 1256 conscious-stricken inquisitors were given absolution if they used instruments of torture. Religion hard at work to save us from ourselves.

Instructions in the 1578 handbook for inquisitors read, in Latin: ". . . so that others would be terrified and weaned away from the evils they would commit." Staunch Catholics regarded the Holy Office as a necessary bulwark against the spread of reprehensible heresies.

The scientist Galileo Galilei had determined, using a telescope, that the earth was not the center of the universe, but that it was a mere satellite in orbit around the sun. Consequently, he was accused of grave heresy. The Establishment, spearheaded by the Holy Roman Catholic Church came down on him in 1615 like a steam roller.

"How *dare* you say that we are not the center of the universe?" The Holy Tribunal, composed of Cardinals, was saying, in effect. "Kneel before us and confess that you are blaspheming, so that we, God's Bible Interpreters, almost God himself, can forgive your grave sins! How can you say that the earth turns and orbits around the sun? Shut up and prevent others from hearing your wicked words. No, we do not want to look through your telescope. It is an instrument from the Devil. Be glad we don't rip the tongue from your mouth!"

Galilei, who knew he was right, halfheartedly confessed to heresy and was sentenced to life imprisonment, modified to permanent house arrest the next day. Thus he remained until his death in 1642. The book he wrote in 1632 about the subject, *Dialogues Concerning the Two Chief World Systems*, was banned by the Church and not until the 1990's—*three and a half centuries later*—was the damnation recanted. As he signed the confession, he was reported to have said, under his breath, "And yet it moves!"—referring to the earth.

While the "Little Ice Age" was going on, from the 15th to the 19th centuries, witches were sometimes blamed for the bad weather and the food scarcity it caused, and were burned at the stake for their crime.

Over the millennia, armies of learned Theologians and Bible Scholars (Scribes and Pharisees) have attempted to rhyme religious dogma with the subject matter in the Book, never realizing that they were studying the *wrong book*. It would have made their task so much easier had they used *Grimm's Fairy Tales* at the outset. They have done their utmost to show us that Religion is a magnificent, glittering temple in which the Creator dwells, but failed to see that what they tried to describe was actually a dusty, snake-infested ruin filled with rot and decay. Maybe that was the reason for the conclusion that there was a great mystery going on.

Misinformation Clearing House/Satan

Organized Religion's Lies came into existence by means of a Governmental/Religious official explanation about what happens after we die. The Ruler was often proclaimed to be either God himself or his legitimate offspring. Priests, appointed by the Ruler, were a big help in explaining that the information came from the Heavens above. This made the message very difficult to ignore.

There is a world of difference between what Organized Religion has to say and the information in the Book. The Book's message is damaging and must be distorted until it is unrecognizable. Organized Religion could be compared with a Misinformation Clearing House (MCH) for itself and Government.

One of the more sinister actions of the MCH is the concealment of the nature of Satan. Why is it necessary to hide his identity? Why does Religion portray him as a monster? Is he really evil?

Concealing Satan's true nature assists Big Government in continuing on its ruinous path of misusing the earth's resources for enrichment and power. Government as well as Religion is benefiting, hiding from scrutiny by this misinterpretation.

Satan is a spirit, invisible, as Yahweh is a spirit. However, the Book describes Satan as an actual being, a fallen angel, who induces mankind to do bad things, like eating the wrong kind of fruit.

By their own inclination, our leaders followed his suggestions. A bad thought or inspiration was put into practice. "He" is therefore nothing more than the wrong spirit, the wrong decision made by our leaders, condoned by us, making all of us equally guilty, although not necessarily equally wicked.

The evil monster sanitized

Showing Satan as the person ultimately responsible for running the world was out of the question. He had to be turned 180 degrees. Organized Religion has seen fit to portray "him" as a monster of nightmarish proportions, and it has managed to scare, confuse and mystify its members for many years. The goat-like, hairy person, a cruel grin on his horned face, knife-like teeth, sulphuric breath, hooves for feet, a stinging tail and a threatening torture instrument in hand is a most improbable character, but he represented fearful reality to millions, who may have had many a sleepless night when they imagined themselves in his devastating grip.

Organized Religion's inspiration

Satan, the actual God of the world and the father of Organized Religion, *likes* to be thought of that way. He *inspired* the explainers of Mystery to this portraiture. Hiding his true personality is fine with him.

The real Satan

Poorly understood about this entity is that we are actually dealing with a handsome, very intelligent, amiable, no-party politician, immaculately dressed in an expensive designer suit, with a winning smile and eyes that say, "Trust me, I won't lie to you!"—a picture of the ultimate used-car salesman; a true charmer. Have you ever asked the question, "Who would want to be seduced by an extremely ugly monster with severe halitosis?" Wouldn't anyone be immediately repulsed by any suggestions such a character proposed? But that's why the switch was made: to pull the wool over our eyes as to his true nature and personality.

The truth is that this guy wants nothing but the best for us. He wants to be our God, instead of Yahweh. He would like nothing better than governing a world with all the countries at peace; preferably with one global, innocuous religion; with one currency; peopled with a healthy, never-dying population, to make good on his lie: "You will not die."

The trouble is that he wants to reach this Utopia on *his* terms. The other trouble is that he really does not know how—his knowledge of how to rule the world falls way short. Wisdom, knowledge and understanding are not found in him, and he refuses instruction from the right source. His idea of government is for the strongest country to impose its will on a weaker one: the rule of the sword. It has resulted in one violent world power after another trying and failing.

And then there is his idea of Religion, which to him is a way to control people. It does not matter to him whether they are Catholic, Muslim or Buddhist, as long as they believe his Big Lie, the one of going to heaven after dying. It may not seem important, but it is, very much so. It is the difference between a right to life and permanent death, about which he'd rather you not find out.

President Eisenhower, leaving office, warned the world about the Military Industrial Complex. It would have been more accurate had he said: "The Military Industrial *Religious* Complex (MIRC), because the acronym is incomplete without the R. Break MIRC down into its individual components and we see what each branch is guilty of:

The *Military* branch is the personification of violence and destruction.

The *Industrial* branch is in charge of using, or misusing, the planet's resources, eventually producing a poisoned environment and even climate changes. The fabulous wealth it creates is used to finance the military machine as well as bribe the law-making government officials.

The *Religious* branch manages to misinform us about most everything.

By mouthing patriotism and heroism, our rulers manipulate us into thinking that, assisted by God, they are working to keep us safe from any enemy.

Well, think again.

There is now, in 2015, a great danger that religion in some parts of the world is poised to take over government again, the way it was when the system of lies was brought into existence. Beware of it; we will see things happen that have never happened before. Neither Christianity nor Islam will be the same again when one or the other gets the upper hand on our planet. There are hard times ahead.

Jehovah's Witnesses and the Book

This book would not be complete without a commentary on Jehovah's Witnesses (JW). Although "Jehovah" is probably not the correct way to pronounce YHWH, it really doesn't matter. What matters is that they claim to have the correct way of looking at the Book (Bible). This is clearly not true, if you take into account what the Book actually says.

There was a time when I thought that the Witnesses had discovered the truth, and were doing the World a great service going door to door, even though they were ostracized practically everywhere, nobly supplying printed matter at no charge to the recipient, matter they had sometimes paid for out of their own pockets. The attraction was that they were a peaceful lot, denounced Organized Religion and refused military service. The Kingdom Halls where they congregated were often no more than simple barn-like structures without frills of any kind. I was charmed—I even went with them one weekend on a door-to-door mission as an observer. However, the rigid reliance on the Headquarters' opinions and conclusions dissuaded me from joining. Evidently I was not cut out to be a member of any group.

The literature they use in their mission is supplied by the JW Headquarters in New York and the witnesses are not allowed to question the contents, or discuss different opinions with those they approach. It appears that the Headquarters' Staff is of the opinion is that most of the statements in the Book must be taken literally, and so they instruct their Witnesses.

One of the publications they distribute these days is a small booklet called "The Bible, What Is Its Message?" In it, several glaring misinterpretations stand out.

Adam's creation is put at 4026 B.C.E., and Eve at some later date. The booklet claims they were childless until after they had sinned, when their first son, Cain, was born. It does not venture to say how old Adam was when Cain was born.

In other JW publications it is stated that Adam and Eve were the very first humans and that all of humanity is descended from this couple. However, Science, using DNA methods, has proven that humans existed many thousands of years earlier.

An interesting archaeological site, Göbekli Tepe, is still being excavated in Southeast Anatolia, in what is now known as Turkey. Many stone structures were found there that were built 12,000 years ago (by carbon dating method), obviously by human hands, using stone-age technology. From the way they are constructed it is clear that the buildings are the result of organized labor and that many hands must have been involved, including design and direction.

Question: If there were no people yet, in 4026 B.C.E., who built those massive edifices?

About the garden of Eden, this booklet says, "God himself planted that garden, filling it with beautiful, fruitful trees." He told them not to eat the fruit of one particular tree, the Tree of Knowledge of Good and Evil. If they disobeyed they would most certainly die. In a recent conversation I had with a JW Elder it became clear that Witnesses have to maintain that the fruit was an actual piece of fruit, although no claim was made as to its exact kind. Eternal life is not mentioned in this Garden of Eden explanation.

The booklet continues with the statement that when Adam and Eve eventually did disobey, "God deferred the death sentence for a time, thereby showing mercy *to their unborn offspring.*" This does not add up for many reasons. In the first place God did not *defer* the sentence—the sentence was not immediate death, but loss of life in the Kingdom. That may be the reason why eternal life was not mentioned. Adam was 930 years old when he died. Eve's age at her death is not mentioned.

In the second place it is hard to believe that Eve did not know what childbearing was, if we take into consideration that The God would "greatly increase the pain of her childbearing" after her act of defiance. Why mention that to a childless woman?

JW's, studying the Book intensively as they do, should know better than peddling misleading thoughts like this door to door.

Without so much as mentioning the slaying of Abel by his brother Cain, the booklet continues with the story of Noah as follows: "As mankind multiplied, sin and wickedness spread rapidly in the earth. Some angels rebelled against Jehovah by leaving their assigned places in heaven, assuming human form on earth and greedily taking women as wives. Unions such as this produced 'hybrid offspring—giant bullies called Nephilim who intensified the world's violence and bloodshed. God was deeply hurt.'"

Actually, the "rebelling angels" are described in the Book as "Sons of God." Question: Who in the Headquarters decided that Sons of God were angels? And where did they come from? Where is heaven anyway? The wives they so greedily took are described as the good-looking "daughters of men." In the absence of other people we are left to conclude that they were Adam's daughters and granddaughters. Question: Is "Adam" the same as "men"?

About the Flood, the booklet says: "The rain came down in torrents for 40 days and 40 nights until the whole earth was submerged. The wicked were gone." There is no scientific evidence that *the whole earth* had been submerged at that period in time.

I have actually confronted several JW Elders with these questions, but have not received a satisfactory answer. It is abundantly clear that questioning the JW Headquarters' interpretations is met with fierce resistance. In that sense this sect resembles Catholicism, where it is unthinkable to question the Pope. The Pope is infallible.

The World today

One of the writers giving his views in the Book in the first century A.D. was the Apostle Paul. He said that our fight was not against *men*, but against *governments and high-placed powers*. Only in recent times, since about the 1970's to 1990's, has it become clear to some observant readers that this man had it right, nineteen centuries ago.

Lately, mainly because of the instant communications of television, radio, cell phones and the Internet, we have been able to observe what used to be secret information for the privileged few: the intrigues, the election frauds, the assassinations, the ruthlessness, the international deals made with Leaders of questionable virtue, the condoned criminality, the interplay between Government, Religion, Commerce, Finance, Medicine and even Organized Crime, and begin to get an inkling of the situation we are dealing with.

No longer can we believe, if we ever did, that Government is here to protect us—we may as well expect the Mafia to do so. It could be that protection was the original thought behind governing, but it has practically always deteriorated into protection *rackets* not all that much different from what the Mafia has to offer.

The not-always-welcome results of Government's governing have lately become very obvious. The spread of uncontrolled pollution, for example, is a direct result of Government's hand-in-glove policy of cooperation with Commerce and Finance.

Money, the root of Commerce, sings a sweet song in the susceptible ears of lawmakers, who need massive funding to be re-elected. The gifts of money prevent them from taking the meaningful measures needed to curb growth and stop the production of toxic waste products which we, and they, eventually eat, drink and breathe.

Growth and Progress is made possible by Religion's constant propaganda of population increase, combined with the efforts of the Medical Profession to keep people alive no matter what.

Climate change is the direct result of Government's interference with the environment and the lack of action to prevent further damage.

The world of Government is like a strong piece of cloth, with woof and warp, consisting of our Leaders and Lawmakers, Religions with their powerful, fear-based hold on people, goods-producing Merchants, financed by legitimate or illegitimate Money, and supplied with customers by Medicine and, again, Religion.

Like a weave, these units interplay, sustain one another and grow rich and powerful together. This world is their playground, with palaces, mansions, yachts, private planes, bodyguards, Swiss bank accounts. And they will fight to the death for their privileged existence regardless of who falls by the wayside. To this end they will consort with criminals, drug dealers, pimps and anyone willing to help them stay up there, in power.

Of course that is not what they do *openly*. In public they denounce crime, and drugs, and prostitution. They lull us to sleep with idealistic prattle they themselves would rather not believe in. They may even announce that they are anti-war, although at the same time they encourage production of huge weapons arsenals, to be sold world-wide. It all helps to keep the money coming in.

A Democratic government may protect sadistic Dictatorships and aid rebels when it seems advantageous. Of course in that case the rebels are called "freedom fighters." At home, it would fight freedom fighters with the utmost force, using police, Army, Navy, or Air Force to either eliminate them or get them back in line.

The Mafia's and Government's aims are not that far apart: their interests often overlap. Government will use Mafia personnel for its less savory jobs, while Mafia figures constantly try, sometimes successfully, to infiltrate Government. That's why there exists in the U.S.A. an Organized Crime Unit, because Government will not tolerate a complete takeover. Not so much because it would be bad for *us*, but because it would be bad for *them*.

The Mafia, of course, cannot openly flaunt an "Organized Government Unit," but we can rest assured that a similar group is an important part of the Mob's make-up. Organized Crime is tolerated as long as it is not an immediate threat to Government.

Therefore there will always be Organized Crime, wherever in the world.

We are pretty powerless against Government, unless we learn to play their game. We can go into politics. We can join the Army and climb up through the ranks. We can choose religion and try to become high-ranking Church officials. We can attempt to become doctors, lawyers, stockbrokers and show our willingness to join. But then we must also learn to be steadfast, and ruthlessly look out for our own interests. Having scruples is dangerous; it may eventually disqualify us. Blowing the whistle almost certainly gets us eliminated from the Circle. The comparison with the Mafia is not so badly chosen: you don't squeal on the Mafia and live; you don't inform on the Government and keep working.

However, if we decide to join them, we should realize that we are joining a lost cause. Even if we vote for our favorite candidate we commit the sin of complicity, because we put our faith in an organization that has had its day, but doesn't have many days left. Apart from the fact that we may live to see its actual end, we may come to regret the day we joined, as we discover that the possibility exists that we are indirectly, maybe even directly, consorting with known criminals.

We do have the option to *ignore* Government, but that isn't easy. And we can ignore it only to a certain extent. Government knows us, knows about us, and knows where to find us. After all, it wants to be financed with part of our earnings, so it keeps tabs. It gives us a number, so that wherever we go it can settle accounts with us.

Our only alternative, really, is to say to ourselves: let them! Let them play their little tricks and games, let them have our money, let them threaten us with their wars and their ridiculous, obscene neutron bombs, let them lie to us from here to eternity—what do we care? We know by now they are strutting around on their last legs. All around us we see the beginnings of the Big Crumble; the end of *their World.*

There may be people who have not been able to see the connection, but the signs are pointing to huge disasters in the relatively near future. Air and water pollution cannot continue on the present scale without causing at least one such disaster. Populations cannot keep on increasing forever; there are limits to how many people the planet will hold. Builders cannot hope to fill every square foot of our planet with buildings, buildings, and more buildings and believe that no repercussions will follow.

Religions will not be able to keep us in dark fear forever; their credibility is rapidly waning. We begin to perceive that they, too, are serving only themselves with their short-sighted interpretations. "Filling the earth" may mean no more to them than filling their churches with humanity and their coffers with the proceeds of *their* particular brand of protection. The question is: if we shouldn't join them and cannot successfully ignore them, what are we to do? Fight them, as Paul seemed to imply 1,900 years ago? Pitching our pitchforks against their atomic weaponry?

In a manner of speaking, yes. Our strength, or the lack of it, doesn't mean a thing, because it will never come to a final physical confrontation between them and us. If it did we'd lose without a doubt. To be sure, they will still manage to kill a horrendous number of us, but they won't be able to kill *all* of us. There will be survivors who will have the pleasure of watching their opponents destroy themselves. They know that the demise is self-inflicted; their continued actions can only lead to this World's collapse.

Our fight is not against *men*. It is against *Powers*. Although men wield those powers, they are not in and of themselves powerful. They are driven to the point of insanity on a collision course with Ultimate Reality. This kind of power can only be fought with words—words of warning, words that reveal, words that point out and set to thinking. Words to wake up our fellow-citizens, maybe some who are even now in power? Words that may make them sweat. Words can be a two-edged sword.

Government officials receive reports, on a daily basis, on environmental problems, to which they outwardly show concern and interest. Either they are not really listening or they have by now realized that there are scant solutions. They may know that environmental deterioration is too far advanced to profit from human interference. They may even see the handwriting on the wall, but will not, cannot, and by their cronies are not allowed to stop doing what they are doing.

It certainly looks as if the end of the World is closer than we may think. The Book claims it will come suddenly, unexpectedly, at a time when everything seems to be running smoothly. The Book claims it will certainly happen, as surely as the sun comes up in the morning and sets at night.

War as a business, a bitter fruit

Because war is a very lucrative enterprise, there now are nations producing the latest, most sophisticated weapons of war as a major part of their Gross Domestic Product. The weapons are sold all over the planet, so that wars can go on in a proper way forever.

It is easy to understand that if the enormous amounts of money and resources now spent on warfare were applied to make a better life for people rather than for an elite few, the situation would be a reverse of the misery any war brings and brighten the future for anyone on the planet.

The country that is now Palestine, described in The Book as "a country overflowing with milk and honey," itself a metaphor for abundance, may have been used to picture the future rich and peaceful situation rather than a few square miles east of the Mediterranean.

Yahweh—in conclusion

The portrayal of Yahweh as the most powerful force in the universe is a running theme throughout the Book. The prophets, thinking deeply about the world around them, discerned that here was a force that had no equal. It was the embodiment of all the laws of nature combined into one entity. A force that caused the universe to exist, beginning eons ago (calculated at 4.5 billion years in 2015—it may be much, much further back in time).

Because nature's laws are unchangeable, the prophets became convinced that Yahweh himself could not have changed over time and decided he was indeed "The one who was, who is and who will be." This led them to the grave conclusion that the World was on its illegal path at its peril. Realizing that the plight the World was in was the result of trying to circumvent nature's laws, they came to the conclusion that nature would strike back and win. It was inevitable.

The God "speaking" to them is not a bad way of presenting their views to their audiences. Their conviction that a huge calamity was in the works was so strong that they may have perceived the various realizations they came to as having been a literal face-to-face meeting with an angry Yahweh.

The God is presented as the one, without exception, who provides food and drink for man and beast. "Even animals in the barren wilderness I supply with water," says Yahweh in the Book. He protects those who are with him and destroys his enemies.

And when it came to Yahweh's way of retaliating they used symbolic expressions such as:

- I will lay waste their cities!
- I will change their pagan festivals into excrement and throw it in their faces!
- I will turn their golden head ornaments into objects of scorn!

- I am rocking the heavens and the earth and the sea and the dry ground.
- I shall certainly overthrow the throne of kingdoms and annihilate the strength of the kingdoms of the nations.
- I will overthrow the chariots and its riders. The horses and their riders will certainly come down, each one by the sword of his brother.

Many references are made to the "dungy idols" of the House of Israel: "I will lay your carcasses upon the carcasses of your dungy idols!"

The reasons for Yahweh's anger are clear: he hates false gods and those who cater to them. Referring to Organized Religion, he states: "Your new moons and your festal seasons my soul has hated. Even though you make many prayers, I have not listened."

The Book, as stated earlier, is definitely an advertisement, a commercial, for Yahweh, The God. In Ezekiel 17:22 he uses a magnificent cedar tree to explain in a symbolic way that he will bring down the high and exalt the low to the benefit of those who are with him. It aims to show that he exists, that he will protect his Israelites, wherever they live, and what he is capable of in terms of destroying his enemies.

One of the dungy idols may be one we do not even recognize as such.

A real theocracy

The recent financial meltdown is the nearest the world has ever come to the visible manifestation of a *theocracy*. Adored and worshipped by the majority of the populace, served by the Wall Street Priests from their obscene crystal temples, the chief God, *Mammon*, reined supreme for a number of ages, only to turn to dust in one month. Mammon's High Priest, Alan Greenspan, confessed that he watched in horror and disbelief as he saw his Deity fall to bits before his eyes and that his familiar past mumblings explaining the workings of his god had become just that: irrelevant mumblings that had meant absolutely zip.

The thing is that it is the invisible gods who wield the most power. We may not realize it, but deities we cannot see may occupy our thought processes and make us behave the way we do. It also means that many real gods exist that are products of our minds, even though most of us will vigorously deny it.

Mammon is one of the false gods, and although there is no such thing as a Mammon statue (maybe a huge dollar or euro sign?) I dare say that he is more real than Baal or Marduk, or any of the thousands of made-up deities in the Babylonian cornucopia.

Worshipping money does not seem to be a religious pastime, but when it becomes a cult, an accepted way of being ruled by its principles (if any), its worship and admiration for the power it exerts is no less real. But because we have no conception of what an invisible god is like, we shrug off the possibility of any such particular deity's existence, oblivious of the fact that there may be consequences of our stance.

Few people think of money as a Religion, or see that there is a connection between gods that are visible and those that are not. Everyone knows that the visible ones, those made of wood, stone, plastic or any material at hand, are powerless statues, even if pronounced powerful by those benefiting by such a statement.

Conventional religion is no exception. We accept that things are the way they are because we have been told by its practitioners that they are. We accept that the incognito "Lord God" is our actual ruler and is with us no matter what, because that is what we hear. We are told that our God is merciful and therefore will never harm anyone. Some of us go to church and sing and pray there because we have been made to believe that is the kind of worship our God requires of us.

We may be wrong.

God or no God, what would it take?

Does God exist? is a legitimate question. There is always the sticky problem that he is invisible, and that makes convincing evidence an impossibility.

The very problem with the above question is that, as soon as the word God is mentioned, immediately, and almost automatically, a connection is made with *religion*. This hampers the effort to come to a reasonable conclusion, because such a connection does not exist. There is no more god in religion than, for example, in atheism or agnosticism. Neither does adherence to such beliefs make someone less moral than religious people. Religion does not have a monopoly on moral behavior.

Atheists are sincere and often have studied religion in more depth than many religious people are willing to go. It is sometimes the very reason it turned them away. Atheist morality and religious morality are non-productive assumptions. It is just as disingenuous as trying to compare an apple to a strawberry. The same goes for agnostics. At least, agnostics may realize that a God exists, but are in doubt, confessing they do not *know*: A-gnostic. Searching for what is true may make one feel uncomfortable at times, but is better to put truth before comfort. It has also been said that sincerity and truth are brothers, but they are not one and the same.

If we want to honestly address the question of the existence of God, the first thing we must agree to is the realization that religion is apt to confuse the issue and cannot be part of the discussion. It would be parallel to suggesting that religious people need a comparison with atheism to prove that they are right in believing that God *does* exist; it is just as disingenuous. All beliefs are open to question.

For now, God is invisible to us. Whether that will ever change is an open question. In our current condition it is just as impossible to point a finger at God as at, say, gravity, or ether.

Invisible things can only be imagined—it is in their nature; they exist in theory only, even God.

God is spirit, a product of the mind. "Seeing" him in this way produces no proof of his existence, nor is it proof of his non-existence if he does not materialize.

It seems that most of us have a need to see God as someone resembling *us*, with a regular body, with facial and other features that are easily recognizable. It may be the reason why he does not want us to make likenesses of him (Exodus 20:4). In spite of that, various allegorical religious artworks, paintings, murals, depict him as the ultimate Father figure with a white beard, on a throne high up in the clouds, touching a recently created Adam with a magical index finger to make him a living being. I presume that in those days clouds were sufficiently distanced from earth to be considered "heaven."

Stephen Hawking

Scientists are generally in denial of a God who was, or is, active in the universe. They demand empirical proof, based on the outcome of their experiments, but, because that has not produced results so far, it was easier to conclude nobody is there, as Stephen Hawking, a famous British scientist and atheist, tries to convince us. However, if scientists cannot even with any degree of certainty agree among themselves what gravity *is*, how can they expect to prove or disprove God? Hawking said at one time that we should appreciate the Grand Design of the universe, as he does, "even if no one designed it." It is obvious that his aversion to Organized Religion is the reason for this astonishing pronouncement.

On a more prosaic note: he realized that the world is in chaos politically, socially and environmentally, but he does not understand why. Nor does he have a solution for the problem. Maybe he belongs to the group of atheists, or even theists, who confuse God with religion. He may wish to look a little deeper into the role of organized religion in the affairs of the world and realize that his imagined God has nothing to do with the unfortunate situation. But maybe he will then come to the conclusion that the Religion he despises *does* have a god, who unfortunately did not create anything but the chaos he is referring to.

Big Bang revisited

The Big Bang, a name only a journalist could come up with, was not an actual explosion, but the result of Zero Entropy. This happens at a temperature at which all molecular motion ceases. Scientists say that a certain ideal gas, cooled to this extreme temperature, Absolute Zero (-273.15 degrees Celsius, or -459.67 Fahrenheit), quickly turns to a liquid, then to a solid, according to the four laws of Thermodynamics. These four laws created the physical universe. Therefore, God = four laws of thermodynamics. The learned men do not speculate where the gas, or the four laws of thermodynamics that made this possible, came from, or if they do, they have not told anyone about it. The assumption is that the gas and these four laws already existed before anything else existed, and without the help of anything or anyone. Really? All by itself, like magic? Maybe God can pull rabbits from hats before rabbits, or hats, even made an appearance. That would make him more powerful than even Stephen Hawking can imagine.

Zero Entropy was the beginning of time, they say. It happened 15 billion years ago. These assumptions make as little sense as appreciating the Grand Design of the Universe coming into existence without a designer. What does Hawking think design is? Does he think that his wheelchair was formed by nature? That the minerals just appeared from the rocks they had been imbedded in and turned without assistance into a frame, a seat, a motor and a battery? Some scientist.

Mentally, we may have to unload a lot of stuff that we have always taken for granted before we can even begin to probe into the deeply hidden truth. It appears that it is not necessary to be learned, wise, or intellectually gifted to grasp the concept of God. Jesus was reported saying that he was thankful to the Father because he had "hidden the truth from the wise [those who think themselves wise, New Living Translation], and revealed to babes [little children, the childlike, NLT] (Matthew 11:25 and Luke 10:21).

The so-called Christian, as well as the Islamic, views of God came to us from prophets. Hebrew prophets named him Yahweh to separate him from other gods; the prophet Mohammed called him Allah, which simply means "the God." The root word here is *Al*, or *El*. It can be identified with El, or Elohim, as in the Jewish religion. Mohammed, claiming he received his revelations to write the Quran from the angel Gabriel, borrowed heavily from the Old Testament. Both religions maintain that the God was the creator of the universe. They never gave us proof of this, apart from pointing out indications of his existence—the abundance of nature, and life itself.

What do we expect? Even if we were on a bus one day, and at the next stop an apparition in a foreign-looking astronauts' uniform with a huge helmet came through the door and the bus driver pointed him out to us: "This is God, he just told me he was the one who created the universe," would we believe it? Why not? It could be the proof we have been waiting for! Think about it.

Some religious people, members of a sect or a "faith", say they can "feel" his presence. They just *know* that he is there, in their church building, with them, listening to their songs and prayers. Either they haven't read Acts 17:24 in their Book, or prefer to disregard the announcement that God does not live in temples made by hands. They may even claim to have a prayer "answered" now and then, solidly convincing them of his existence. It doesn't prove anything. The fact that something is popularly accepted as holy truth does not mean it is good and trustworthy.

The God who comes through in the Book does not "answer" prayers. He isn't even listening. It would come down to doing somebody a personal favor, which he does not do. The only prayer he apparently accepts is the one where we, the earth's inhabitants, as a group, ask him to free us from the *world's god*, who is still misleading us on a grand scale, creating havoc, and the main influence in the barrage of misinformation that keeps us from finding out who God is. Maybe, if there is a God, he wants his chosen people to be around for much more than three-score-and-ten years, eternally, as he calls it, so that they will have enough time to get to know him. And as an added bonus, find out a few things about the universe, the earth, ourselves and the fruits of Eden.

It is my sincere hope that this publication will lead to a better understanding of the Book, what the World is about, why religion exists in the form it does, what real worship entails and why we don't really have to be afraid of a Devil and his supposed hell. The nightmare never existed, and we should feel strong compassion for the millions who in the past were forced to become its victims.

S.P.

SOME EXPLANATIONS

The snake and his strange punishment, or the fate of Satan

As we understand that the snake, or serpent, is the symbol for the god of this world, it is clear that, if he will be "crawling on his belly and eating dust," it means that he, in the end, will be humiliated and forced to admit that his take-over has failed. His world has turned to dust and that is what his food will be from now on.

He will also be *jailed* during the thousand-year Kingdom **). This means that he will not be dead yet, but won't have any influence on the "Israelites" populating it. One could say they are cured of him.

The jailing of Satan is pictured with an angel coming down from heaven with a key to the abyss (jail) and a chain to put Satan in there for 1000 years. (Rev 20:1-3), together with the Beast and the false Prophet, who are already in it (19:19).[6] After the jail period he will be set free for a short time to give him one last chance to establish his rule. The population will have increased by then, with some who have not known him and may be tempted, but they will also be told, as we are now, to shy away. The knowledge tree will still be there, and its fruit available.

It is explained that anyone he *does* get to follow him at that

---

[6] The thousand years may not be an exact time span, but a figure of speech: a stretch of time, an epoch long enough to return the earth to its original pristine condition, and for his "Israelites" to enjoy peace and security for a change. A "day" in Yahweh's scheme of things.

time will be subject to the "second death," which is final. No parole. The original "Israelites," however, will not be subject to this second death, as they have "eternal life."

After his second attempt has also failed, Satan will be killed, never to appear again.

This is symbolically pictured in Revelations 19, 20 and 21, by John of Patmos.[7]

In 20:11 and 12 all the dead are being judged, some to live, some not. The Book calls it the first resurrection.

After this Satan must be let loose for a little while and mislead the nations again. He'll assemble a huge army to make war with the "holy ones" but will not succeed. (Symbolic) fire comes down from heaven and devours them. Second death. Second resurrection. Anyone not qualifying goes into the lake of fire (20:15). Not to be tormented forever, but to be eliminated forever.

20:6 tells about the second death (the lake of fire) having no authority over those who survived the first death.

In Daniel 7 the Kingdom is described as "for time indefinite upon times indefinite."

Revelations 20:10 describing Satan's final end

In 20:14, death, as well as the grave, go into the lake of fire. Death is no more.

22:12 tells who will be allowed to enter the City. (The holy city of Jerusalem, symbol for the Kingdom, and Life.)

21:27: Anything not sacred and anyone that carries on a disgusting thing and a lie will by no means enter it.

It seems that the prophets, perhaps unavoidably, often used the same symbolism (beasts with horns, sometimes horns with eyes and mouth, clothing white as snow, a giant wheel with eyes all around) when describing future events or situations. John

---

[7] John of Patmos was not from Patmos, but is called so because he cannot be identified any other way. He was on the island when he wrote Revelations. It is probably not John the Apostle.

obviously used portions of Ezekiel, Daniel, Psalms and Isaiah, although he does not identify his sources anywhere. It is therefore problematic to see him as someone receiving information directly from Jesus, as he claims.

Some of it, however, does not seem to have connections with other prophets. When he talks about the eventual fate of Satan, or the time after the 1000-year Kingdom, when the Liar is let loose on the world again, it seems to be original information, unless he had access to sources we don't know about. He may have thought deeply about what he had read earlier and drawn his own conclusions. That, generally, is what prophets *do*.

Again, it is up to the individual reader to decide if the proffered possibilities are reasonable or not.

In the light of Yahweh being fair and just, he must give Satan every opportunity to prove his case. Also, by doing it this way, he makes sure that the final outcome will be without any doubt satisfactory to himself, his Israelites and even to Satan, who, while crawling on his belly and eating dust, will have to admit that Yahweh is indeed more powerful than anyone, or anything, in the universe. He has no grip on the original "Israelites" of the Kingdom. He can only try to charm the new crowd that accumulated after the first millennium, but they will have been cautioned by their fellow citizens as to what he stands for. Losing all his influence may be the symbol for Satan's final annihilation: his "death."

In the end it all comes down to a change of mind.

THE END

BIBLE REFERENCES OF INTEREST

1 Cor. 8:15 (many gods)
Deut.7:6 (holy = special)
John 5:27 (about death)
Matthew 5:5 (The meek . . .)
Eccl. 9:5-10 (the dead know nothing)
Psalm 6:5 (no remembrance of you)
Eccl. 3:19 (One breath for man and beast)
Psalm 146:4 (Thoughts perish)
1 Cor. 15:26 , 15:54 (Last enemy, death . . .)
Dan 7:13, 14, 27 (Kingdom)
2 Cor. 11-14 (Satan, angel of Light)
2Cor.4:4 (God of this world)

ACKNOWLEDGMENTS

Thanks to my daughter, Saskia Raevouri, who graciously agreed to publish this book even though she has New Age beliefs which are not in harmony with the contents of *my* book.

Also to Matthew Block, her American husband, who became a Dutch citizen and is now better versed in the language of Holland than most Hollanders. He has been a great help in proofreading both versions and made valuable suggestions for sequencing.

www.ingramcontent.com/pod-product-compliance
Lightning Source LLC
Chambersburg PA
CBHW031446040426
42444CB00007B/999